MODERN ARBAN-ST. JACOME
Comprehensive Course for Trombone or Baritone

THE *Modern Arban-St. Jacome*, a comprehensive course for trombone or baritone, bass clef, represents a compilation of two of the world's most famous brass instrument methods, completely revised, re-edited and re-styled to meet the demands of modern education. The original editions of these justly celebrated works, abounding in a wealth of valuable material that for over half a century proved itself indispensable in brass instrument study, were written at a time when teaching procedures were quite different from what they are today, and as a result, any attempt to make use of them in our present scheme of education inevitably results in a multitude of problems confronting students and teacher alike. Originally intended for pupils whose interests were paramount enough to justify them giving their full attention to music study, the original versions of these great works advance in strides far too rapid for most students. Furthermore, the material as presented in the original dress of these two methods is not graded progressively; the first pages of each book are of a difficulty far beyond most beginners, and when proceeding through the two methods it is found that while the musical content is easy enough to digest in some places, in others it is completely out of bounds for those at that particular stage of advancement. Furthermore, melodic material in the form of well-known melodies, which is so necessary in sustaining students' interest while developing the mere mechanical aspects of musical performance, hardly exists among the pages of either Arban or St. Jacome. These facts convinced the writer that time was opportune for a complete revision and adjustment of the two greatest of all brass instrument methods, in order to bring them to a place where they could be of some real service to the students of today as well as being adaptable to either individual instruction or the class method plan of teaching.

IN the present volume the writer has directed all efforts toward modernizing and improving the original versions of Arban and St. Jacome. Many new and worthwhile studies and exercises have been incorporated into the work, and in places, complete new sections have been added, given over to such problems as hitherto remained in the background. Many familiar melodies have been interspersed throughout the array of technical material, and each of the most frequently played major and minor keys is taken up in a systematic, logical fashion. Throughout the whole of *Modern Arban-St. Jacome*, constant stress is made of the absolute necessity of (1) the regular practice of long, sustained tones, which are in themselves of prime importance to all in developing *strength* of lip muscles, and (2) the regular practice of interval and lips slurs, which likewise are of prime importance to all in developing *flexibility* of lip muscles.

THE current work is admirably suited for class instruction in schools and its use therein will bring to the young musicians of America an opportunity to profit from the study of valuable teaching materials, devised and written by two of the greatest teachers the world ever has known, but which hitherto have been inaccessible to a large number of students due to their former manner of presentation.

AS a companion book to the *Modern Arban-St. Jacome* method for trombone or baritone, the writer has prepared a completely revised and modernized edition of the famous Pares exercises for trombone or baritone, which is titled *Modern Pares* and is published by Rubank, Inc. It is strongly urged that students, when they have studied as far as page 62 in the present work, be introduced to the worthwhile scale and foundation studies of Pares, these two books being used in conjunction with one another from there on.

IF the *Modern Arban-St. Jacome* method for trombone or baritone proves itself a boon to those in quest of material to aid in solving the many problems that confront the present day instructors of trombone and baritone, whether they be private teachers of these instruments, or public school music directors, the writer will feel gratified to know that his earnest efforts have been of at least some educational significance.

Harvey S. Whistler, Ph. D.

Position and Fingering Chart for Trombone and Baritone

TROMBONE POSITIONS ABOVE NOTES; BARITONE FINGERINGS BELOW NOTES

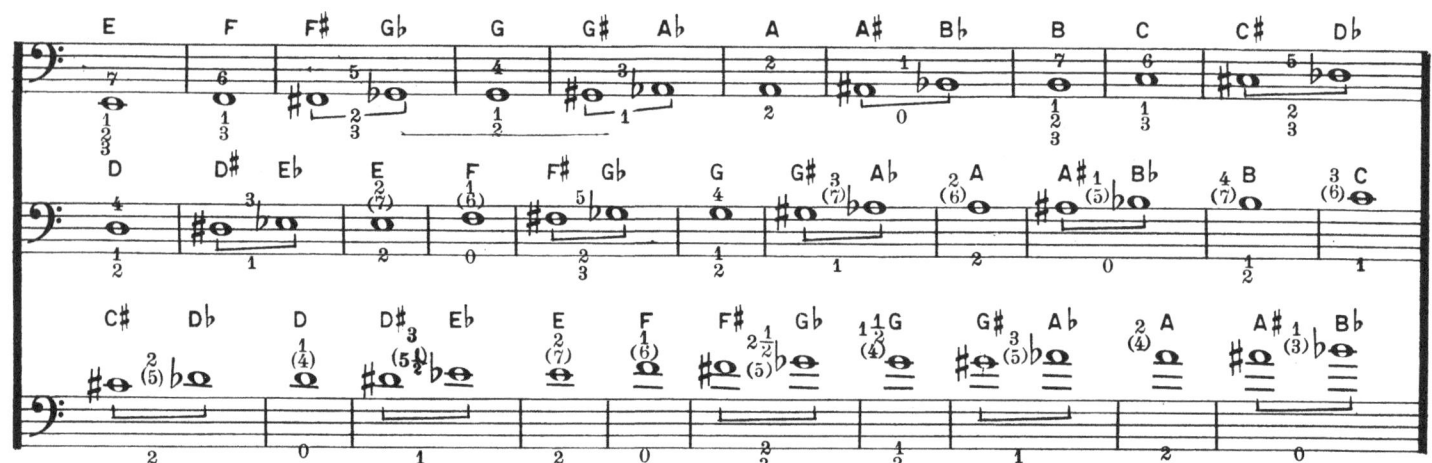

Altissimo register   Trombone pedal tones

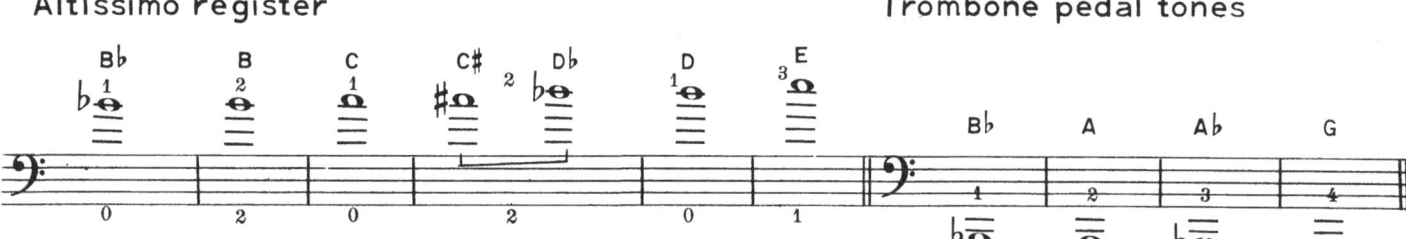

Table of Harmonics

Preliminary Lesson

Starting on "Low B♭"
For students finding it necessary to begin on this tone

Whole Note (o) = Four Counts — Whole Rest = Four Counts
Trombone positions above notes; Baritone fingerings below notes

Preparatory Studies

THE FIRST TONES

Whole Note (o) = Four Counts — Whole Rest (≡) = Four Counts
Trombone positions above notes; Baritone fingerings below notes

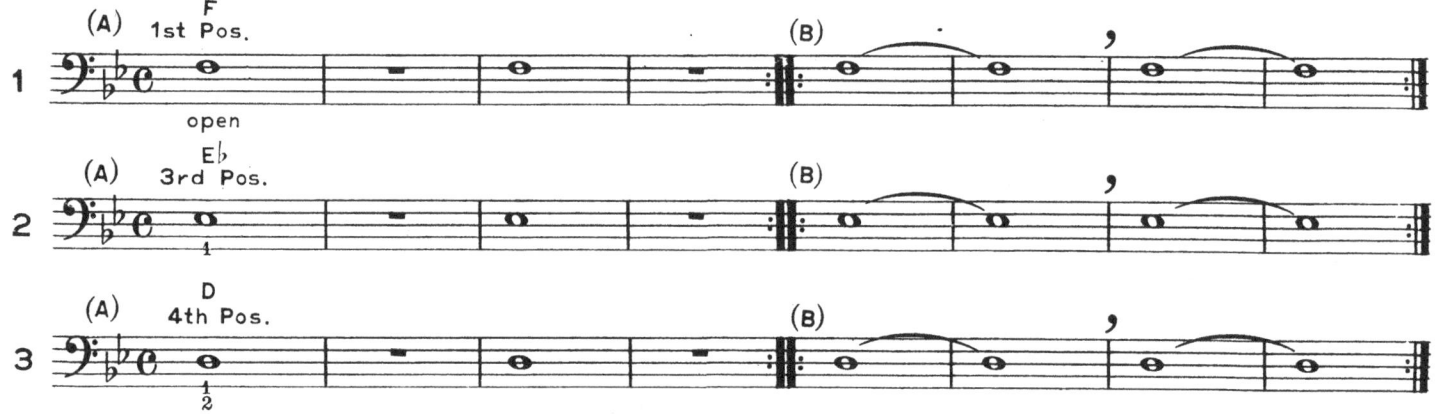

TECHNIC BUILDER

LONG TONES TO STRENGTHEN LIPS

EXTENDING THE RANGE DOWNWARD

TECHNIC BUILDER

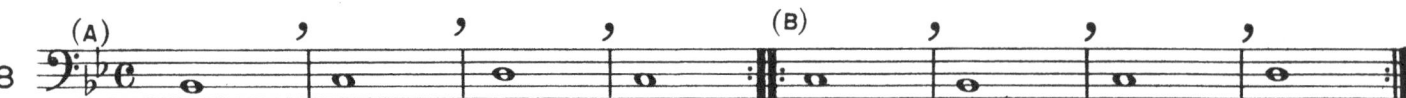

FOUNDATION STUDIES

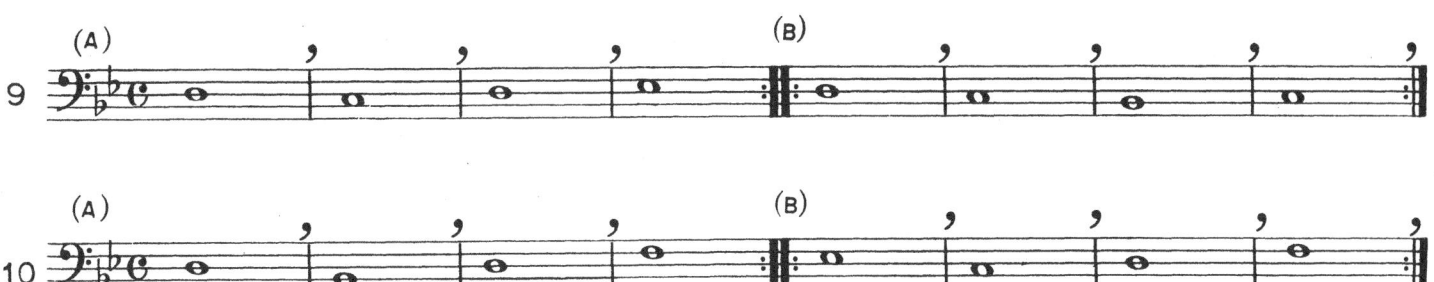

INTRODUCING A NEW TONE

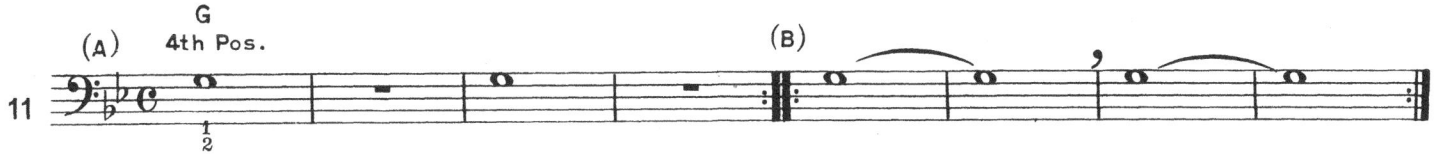

TECHNIC BUILDER

FOUNDATION STUDIES

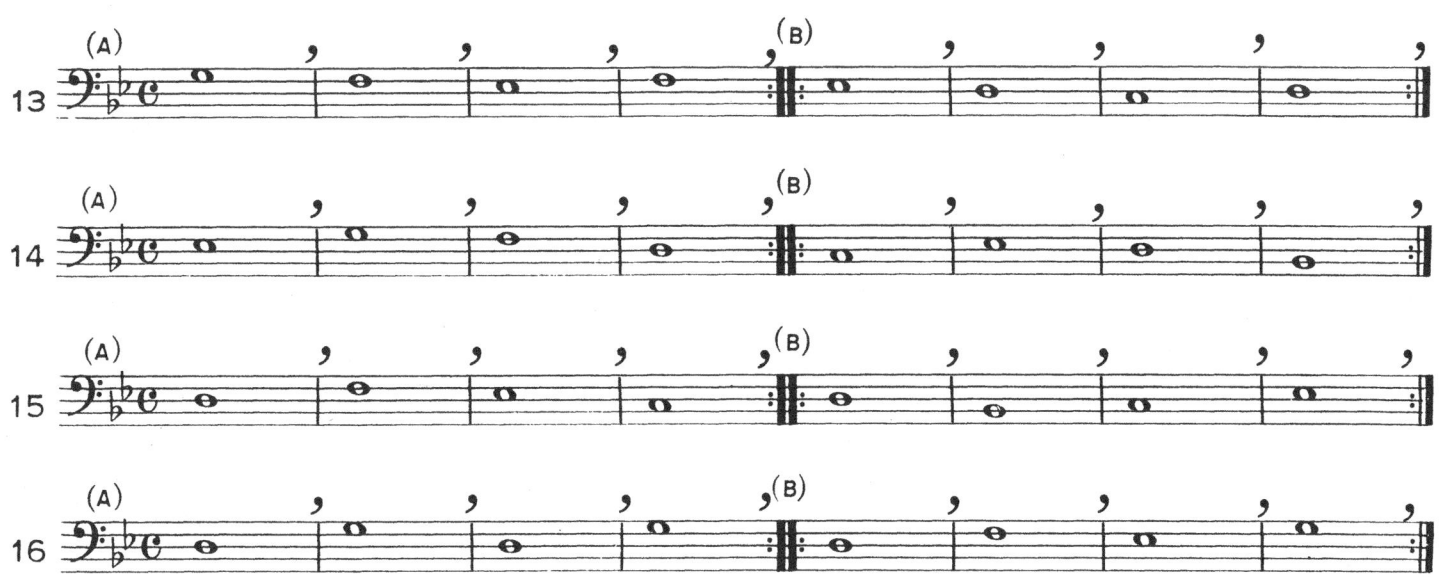

LONG TONES TO STRENGTHEN LIPS

INTRODUCING HALF NOTES and HALF RESTS

Half Note (♩) = Two Counts — Half Rest ■ Two Counts

HALF NOTE EXERCISE

SLURS

ANOTHER HALF NOTE EXERCISE

MORE SLURS

TONE BUILDER

Favorite Melodies

Introducing 2/4 Time (Meter)

EXERCISE

STUDY

OPERATIC THEME
VERDI

THE CHATTERERS
OFFENBACH

Introducing ¾ Time (Meter)

Technical Studies

DEVELOPING LIP FLEXIBILTY AND STRENGTH

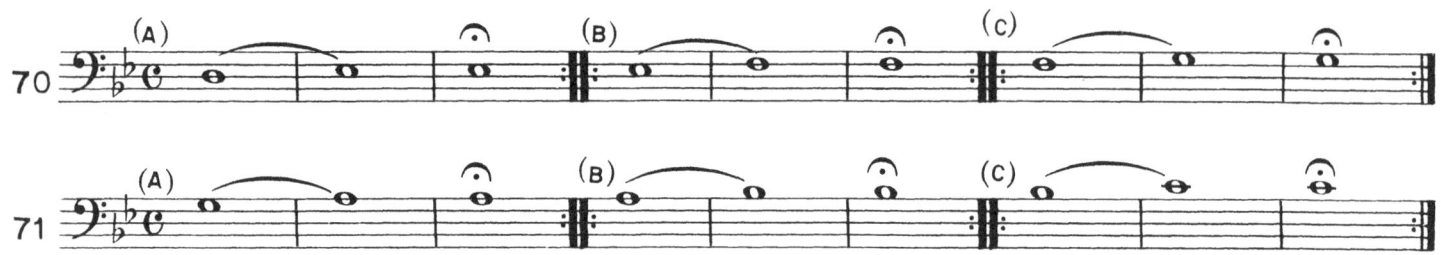

DEVELOPING "D"

D *This tone often is too flat. To correct this, use 4th position on Trombone, and 1st and 2nd valves on Baritone.*
1st Pos.

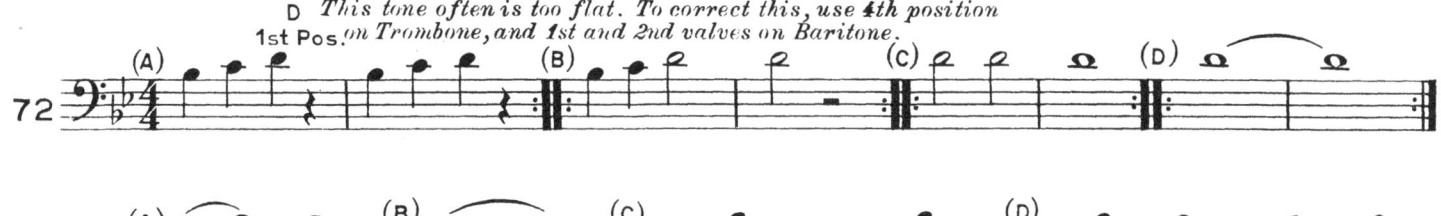

BASIC STUDY

Baritone practice slurring each two measures.

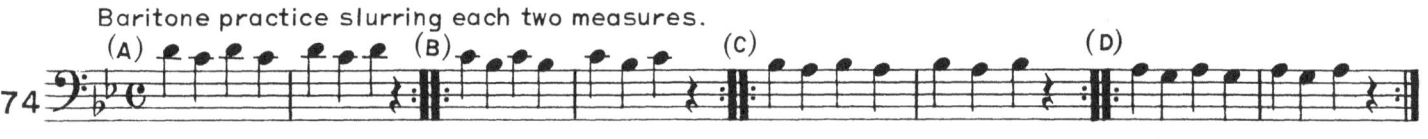

ETUDE

Baritone practice slurring each two measures.

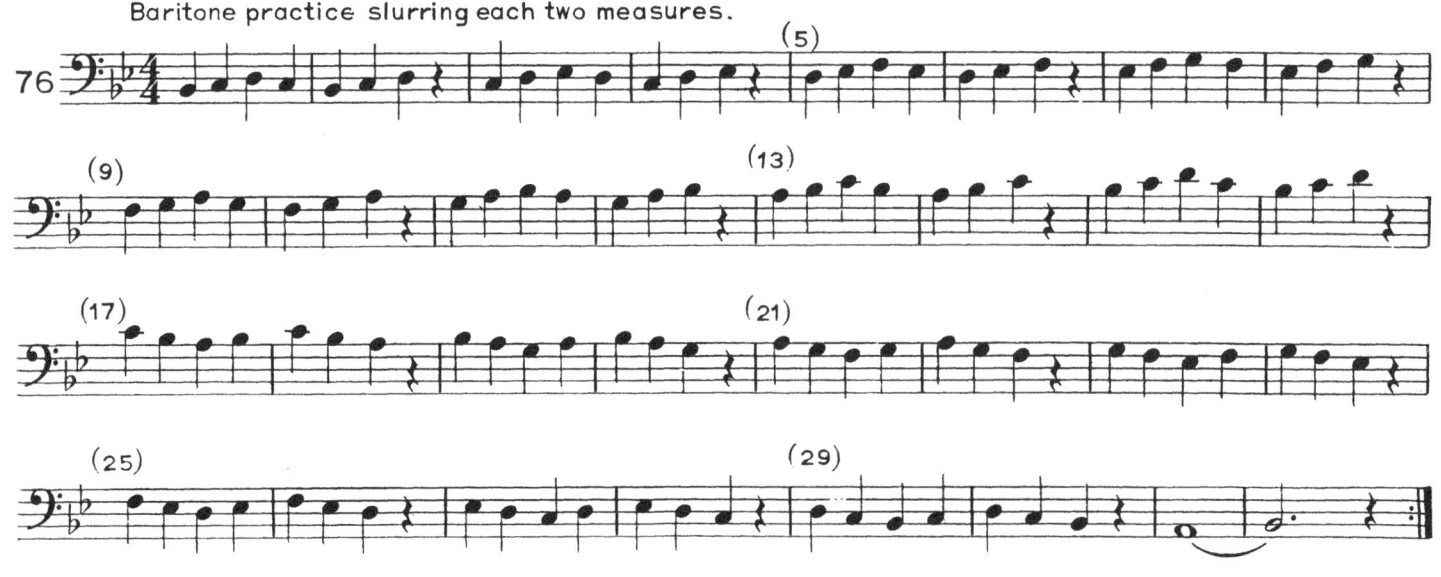

Rhythmical Studies

Key of C Major

Also practice very slowly, holding each tone for (1) FOUR counts and (2) EIGHT counts.
When playing long tones, practice (1) ⋖ and (2) ⋖⋗.

SLURS

Also practice very slowly, holding each tone of each slur for FOUR counts.

DEVELOPING "E"

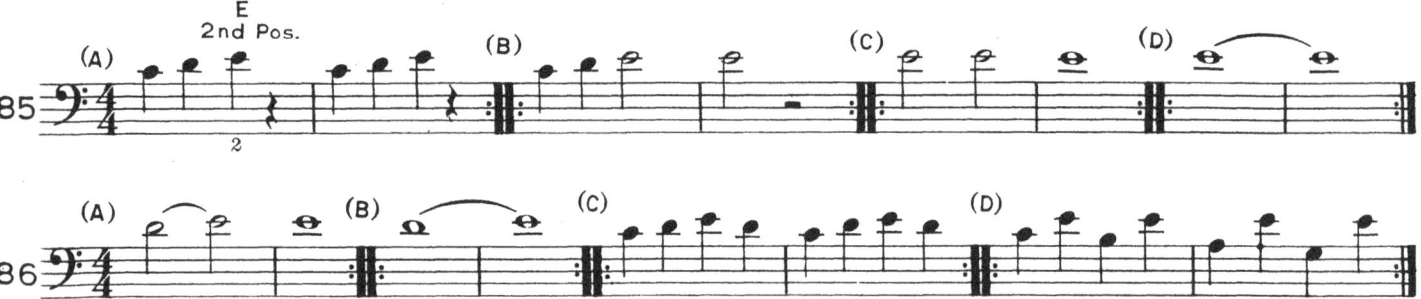

SCOTCH AIR

Traditional

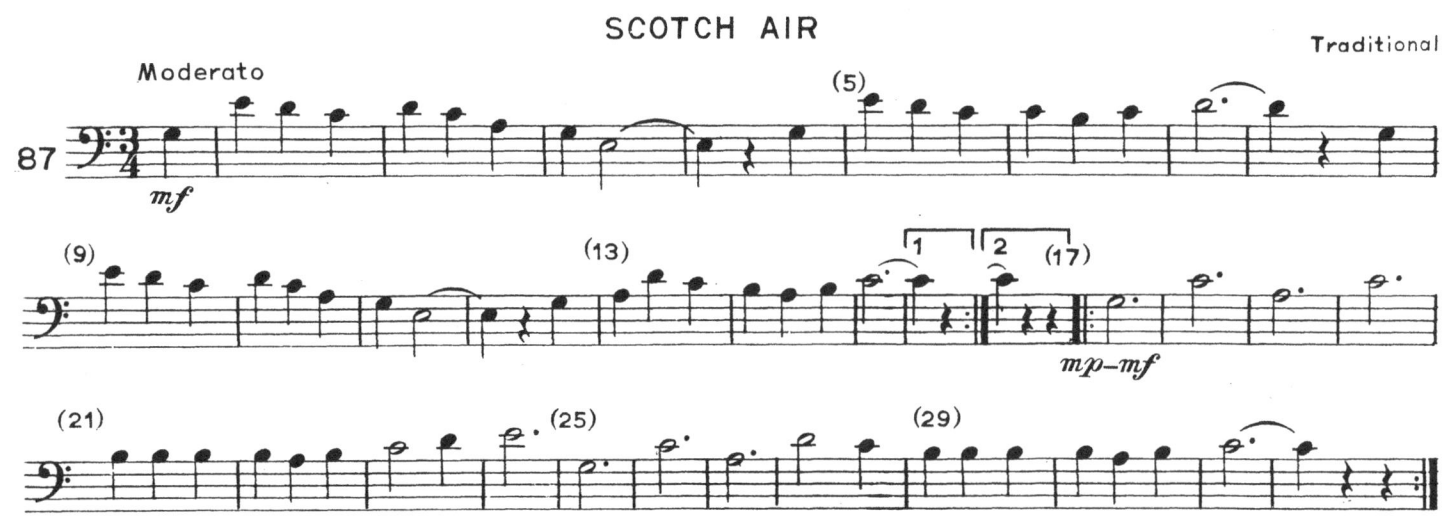

INTRODUCING THE DOTTED QUARTER NOTE FOLLOWED BY AN EIGHTH NOTE

88

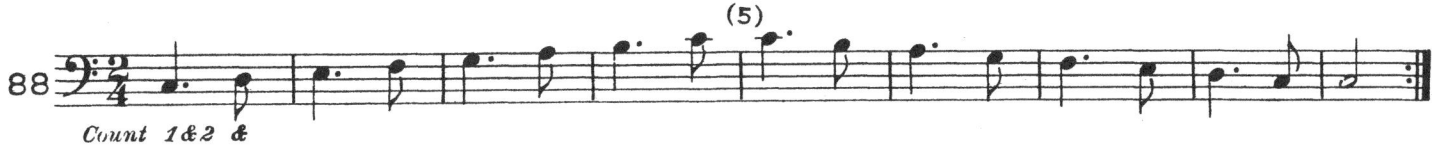

OLD WELSH MELODY

Traditional

Con spirito

89

Largo from New World Symphony

DVORAK

Legato e sostenuto

90

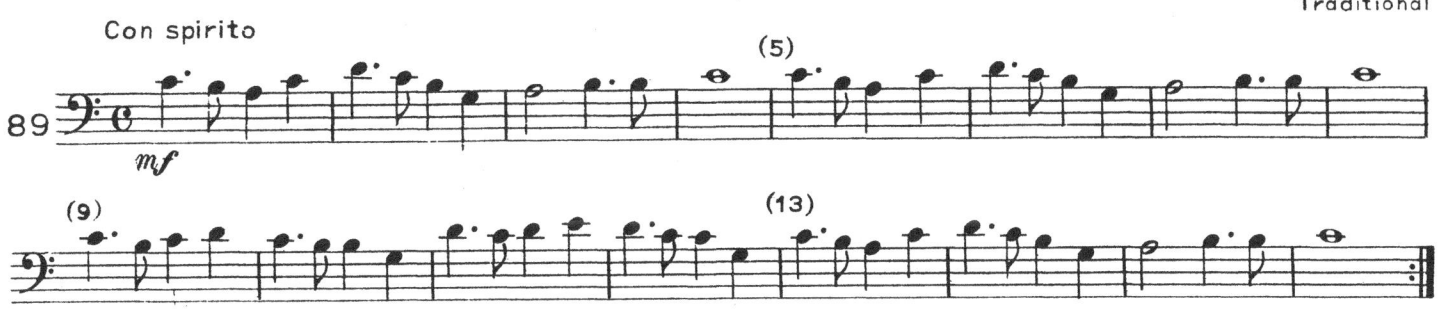

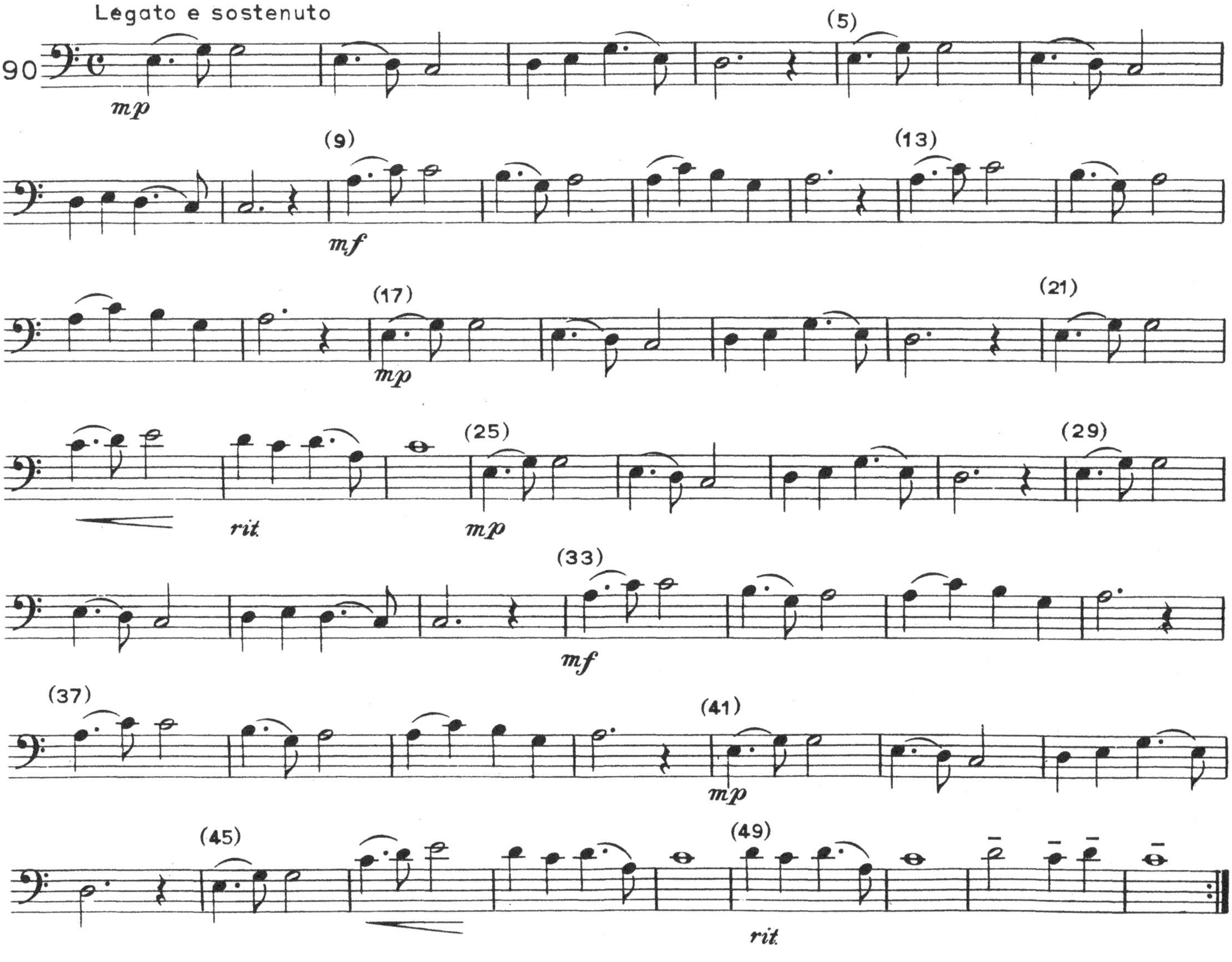

Key of F Major

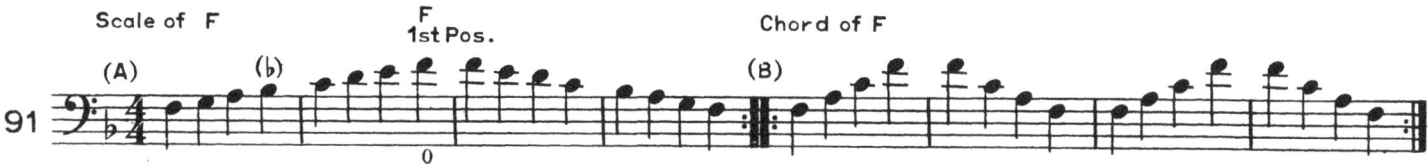

Also practice very slowly, holding each tone for (1) FOUR counts and (2) EIGHT counts.
When playing long tones, practice (1) — and (2) —.

SLURS

Also practice very slowly, holding each tone of each slur for FOUR counts.

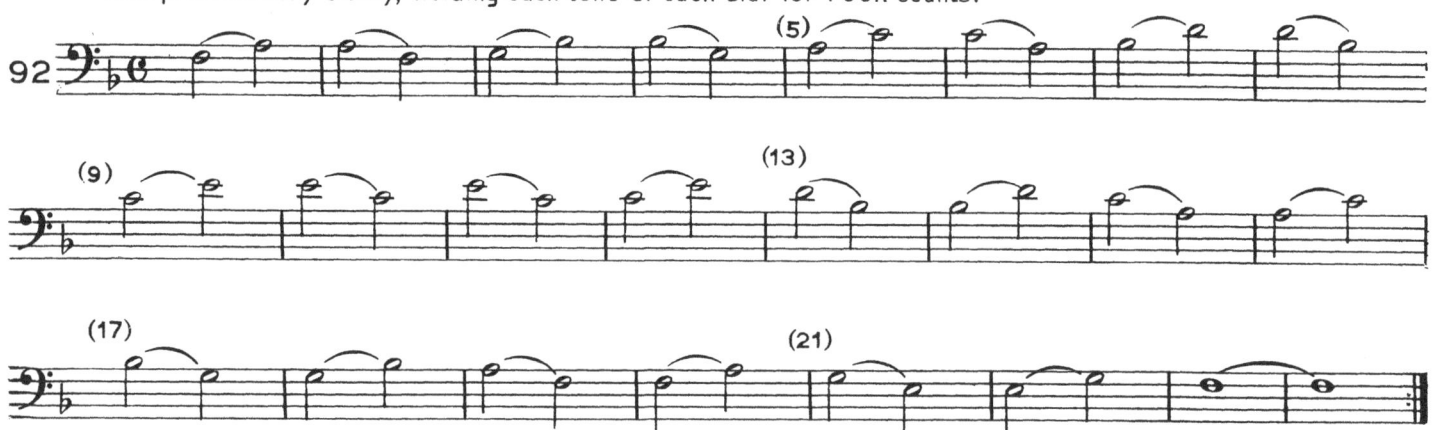

PIONEER SONG

DEVELOPING "F"

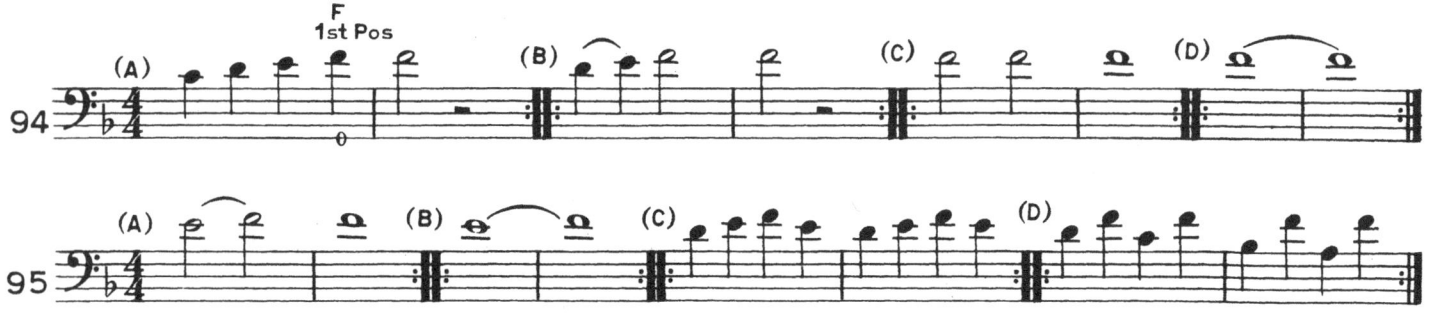

Introducing 3/8 Time (Meter)

THEME

Introducing 6/8 Time (Meter)

Drink to Me Only With Thine Eyes

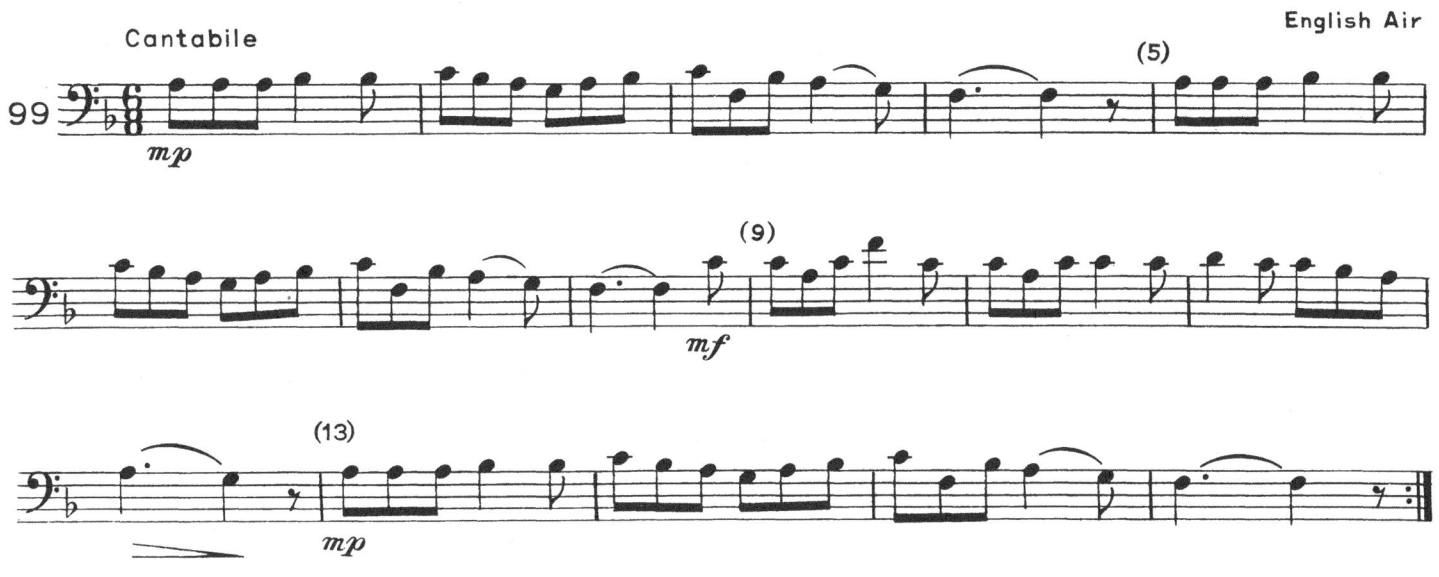

Key of G Major

Also practice very slowly, holding each tone for (1) FOUR counts and (2) EIGHT counts.
When playing long tones, practice (1) < and (2) <>.

SLURS

Also practice very slowly, holding each tone of each slur for FOUR counts.

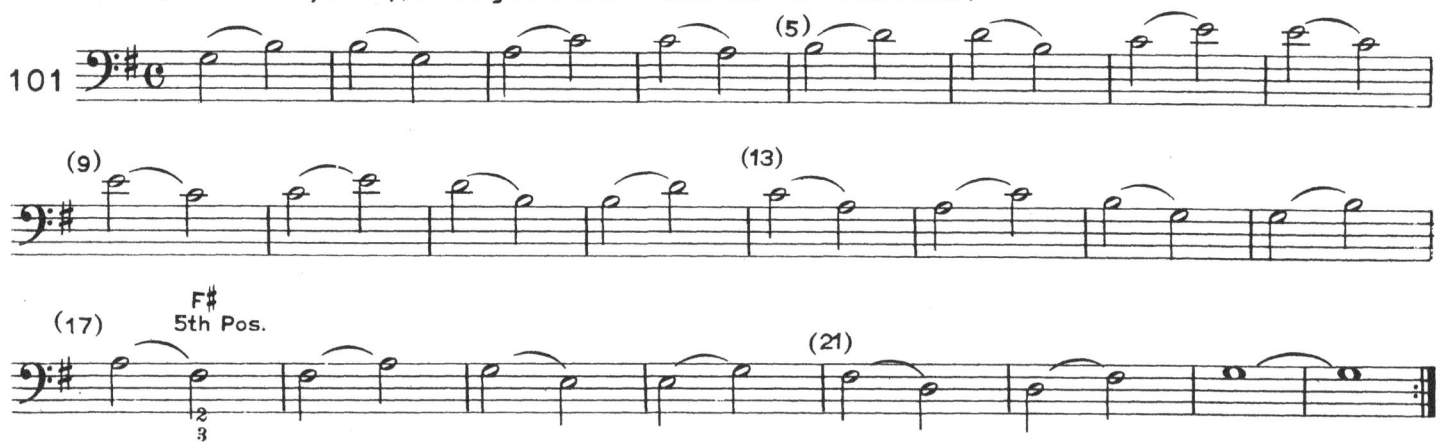

SHORT EXERCISES EMPLOYING "MIDDLE F#"

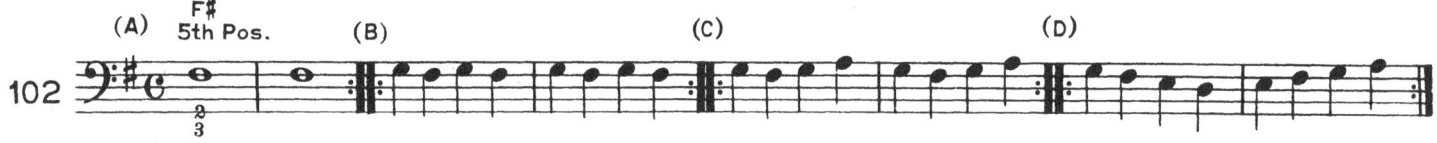

On Wings of Song

MENDELSSOHN

ANDANTINO
LEMARE

DEVELOPING "HIGH F#"

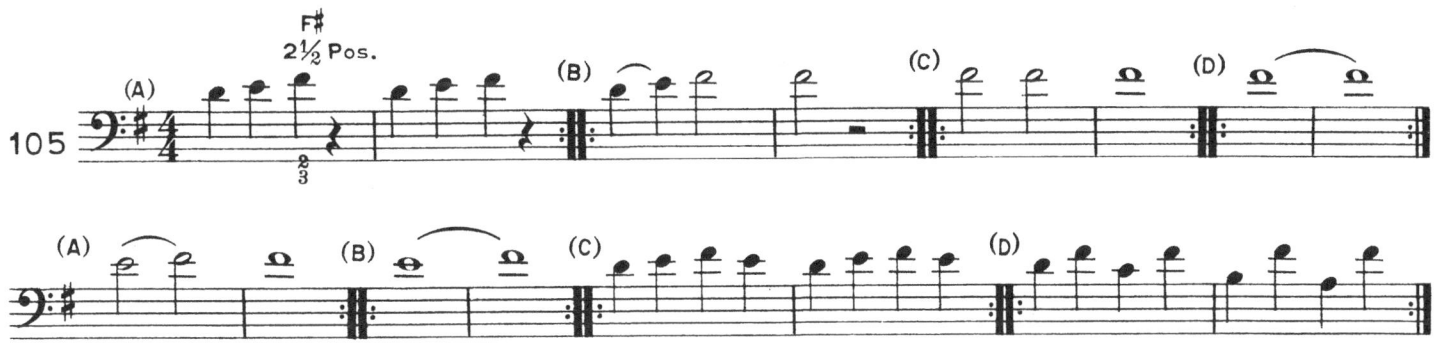

DEVELOPING "HIGH G"

Melody from Oberon
WEBER

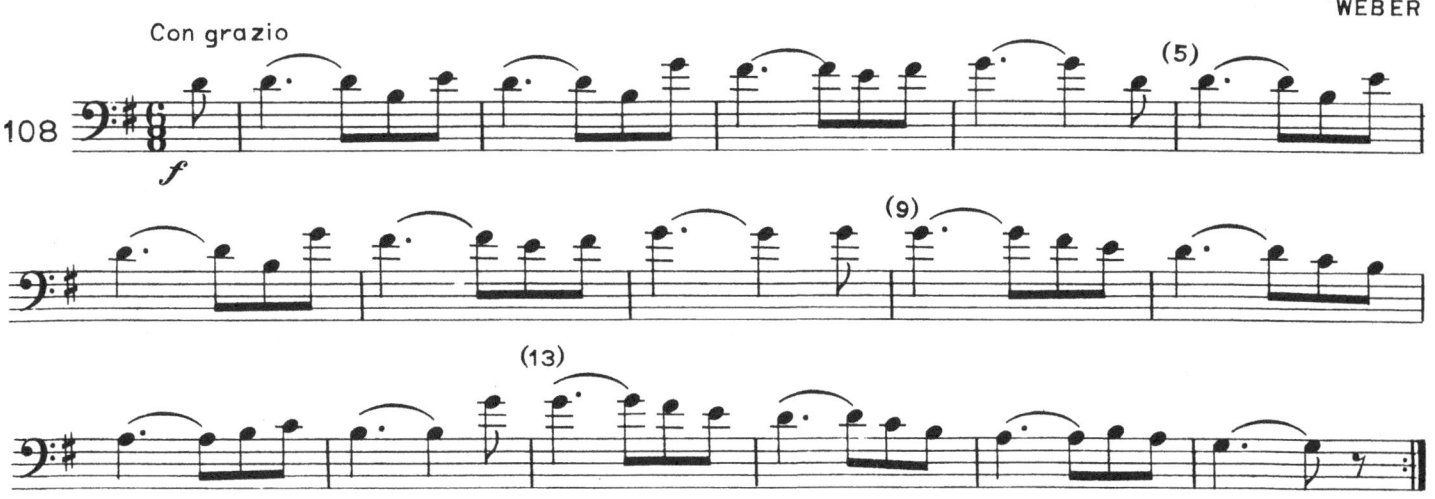

Key of B♭ Major

Also practice very slowly, holding each tone for (1) FOUR counts and (2) EIGHT counts.
When playing long tones, practice (1) $<$ and (2) $<\;>$.

SLURS

Also practice very slowly, holding each tone of each slur for FOUR counts.

SHORT EXERCISES EMPLOYING "LOW B♭"

SONG WITHOUT WORDS

MENDELSSOHN

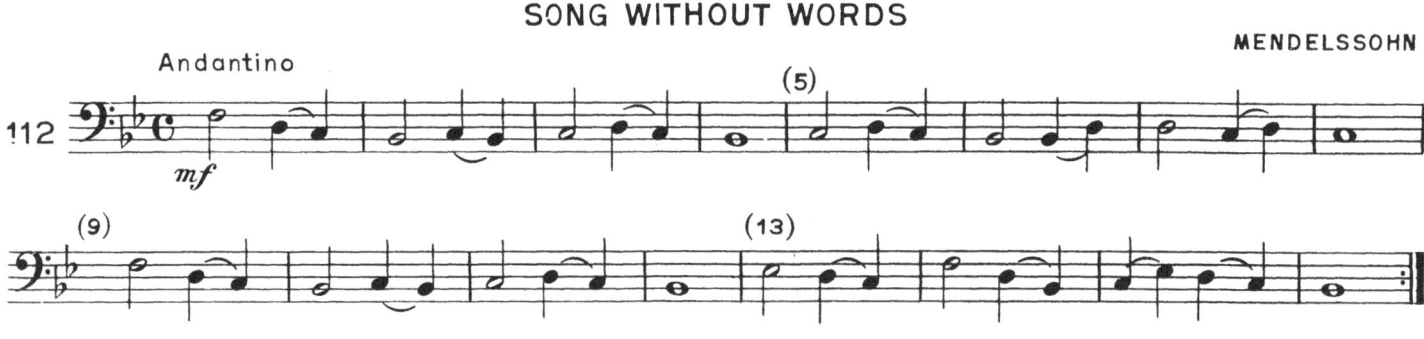

HANSEL and GRETEL

HUMPERDINCK

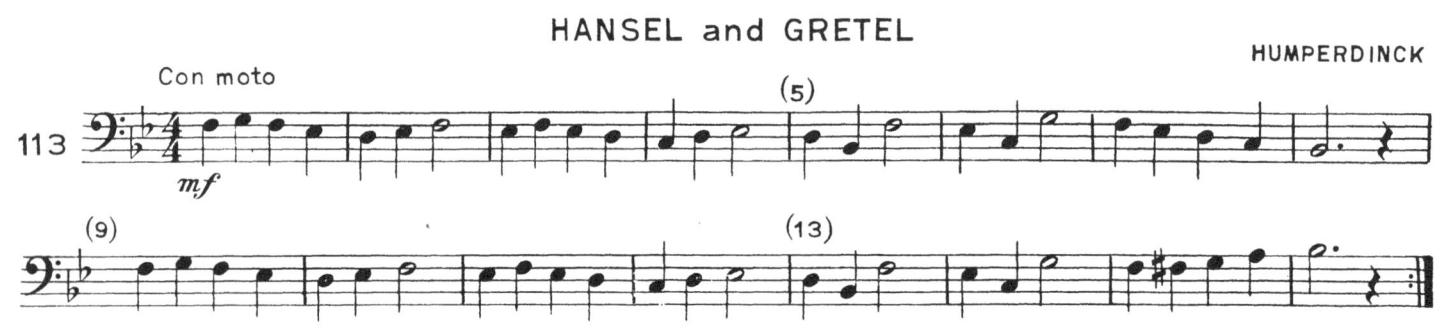

INTRODUCING "High E♭"

ADESTE FIDELIS

Traditional

ANVIL CHORUS
from Il Trovatore

VERDI

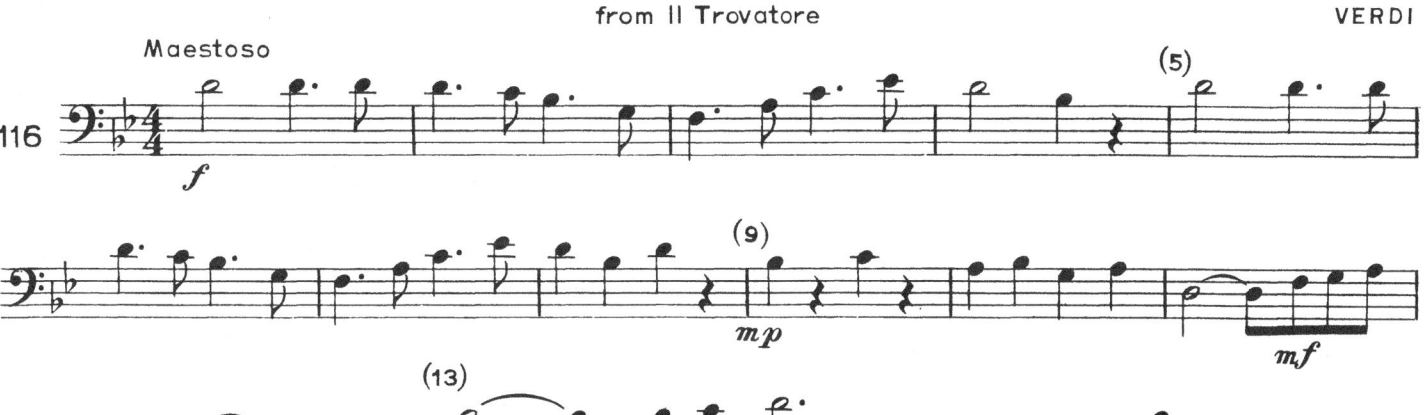

AULD LANG SYNE

Scotch Folk Song

Key of D Major

Also practice very slowly, holding each tone for (1) FOUR counts and (2) EIGHT counts.
When playing long tones, practice (1) $<$ and (2) $<\,>$.

SLURS

Also practice very slowly, holding each tone of each slur for FOUR counts.

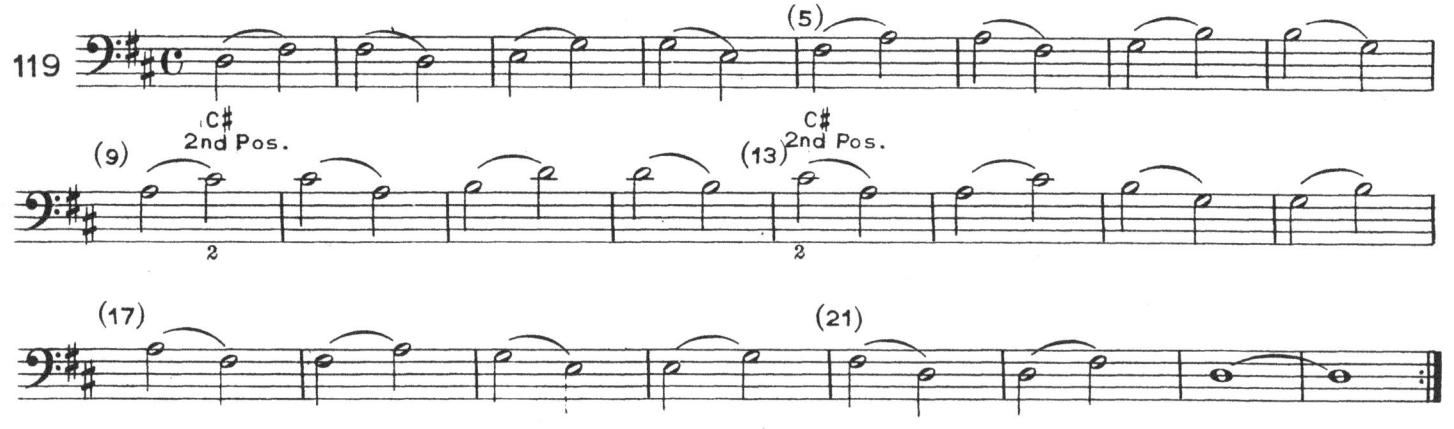

INTRODUCING "LOW C#"

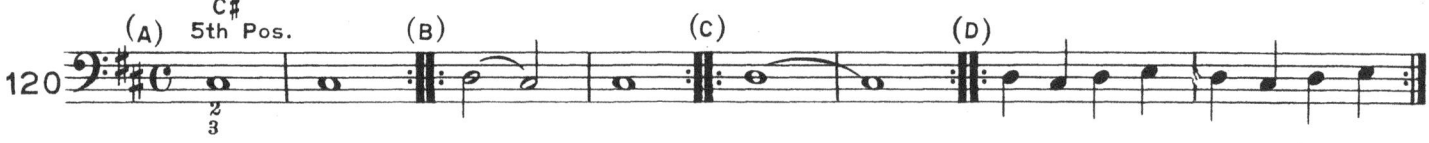

VALSETTE in D

J. LEYBACH

FRENCH FOLK SONG

Traditional

INTRODUCING STACCATO

DEVELOPING THE STACCATO

STACCATO STUDY ON THE SCALE

STACCATO EXERCISE

EIGHTEENTH CENTURY THEME

MOZART

Key of E♭ Major

Also practice very slowly, holding each tone for (1) FOUR counts and (2) EIGHT counts.
When playing long tones, practice (1) $<$ and (2) $<\!\!>$.

SLURS

Also practice very slowly, holding each tone of each slur for FOUR counts.

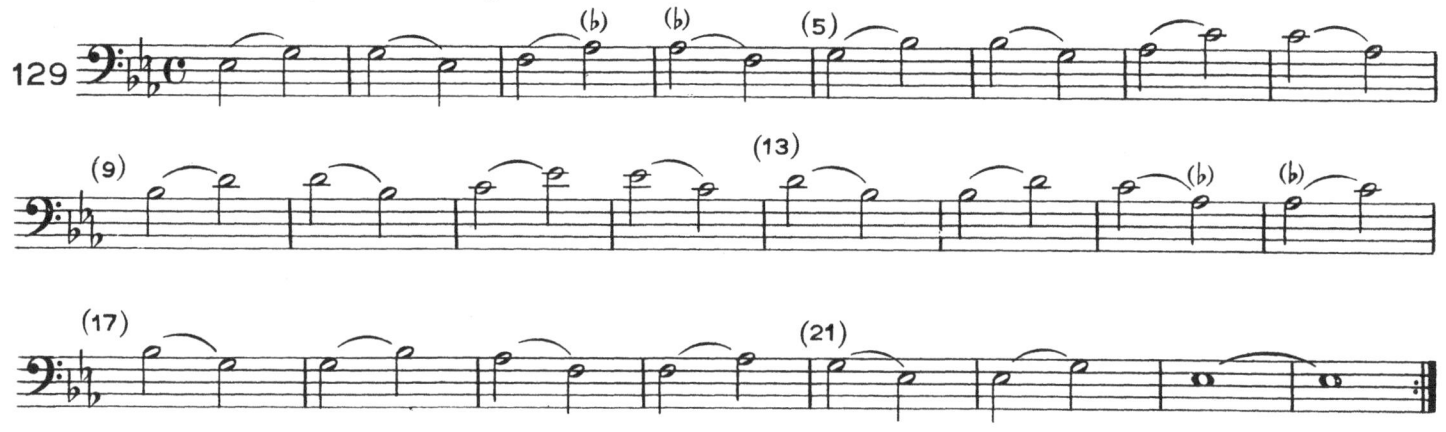

STACCATO EXERCISE ON THE SCALE

STACCATO STUDY

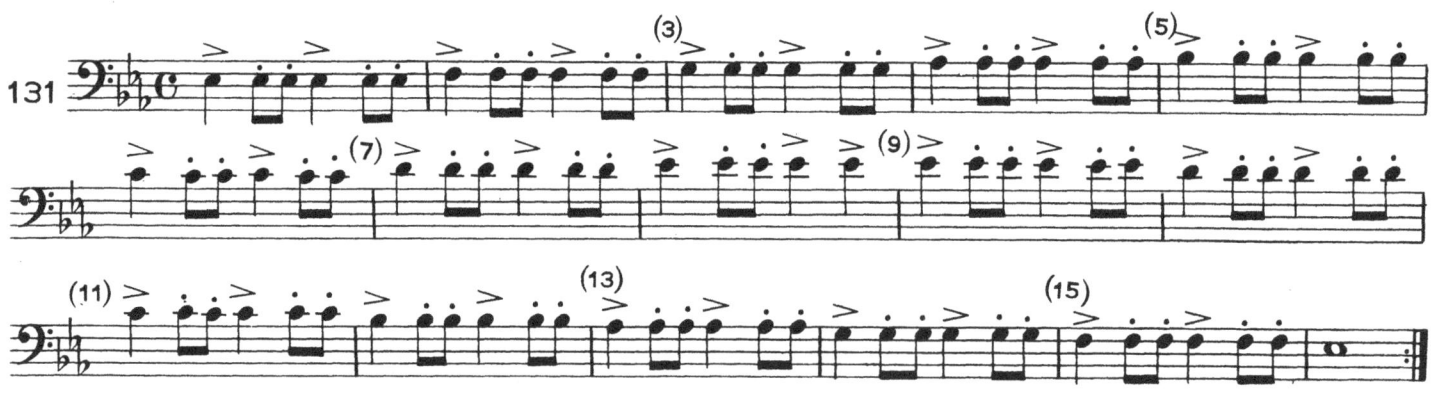

THEME from AMARYLLIS

H. GHYS

AIR from DER FREISCHUTZ
WEBER

Skater's Waltz
E. WALDTEUFEL

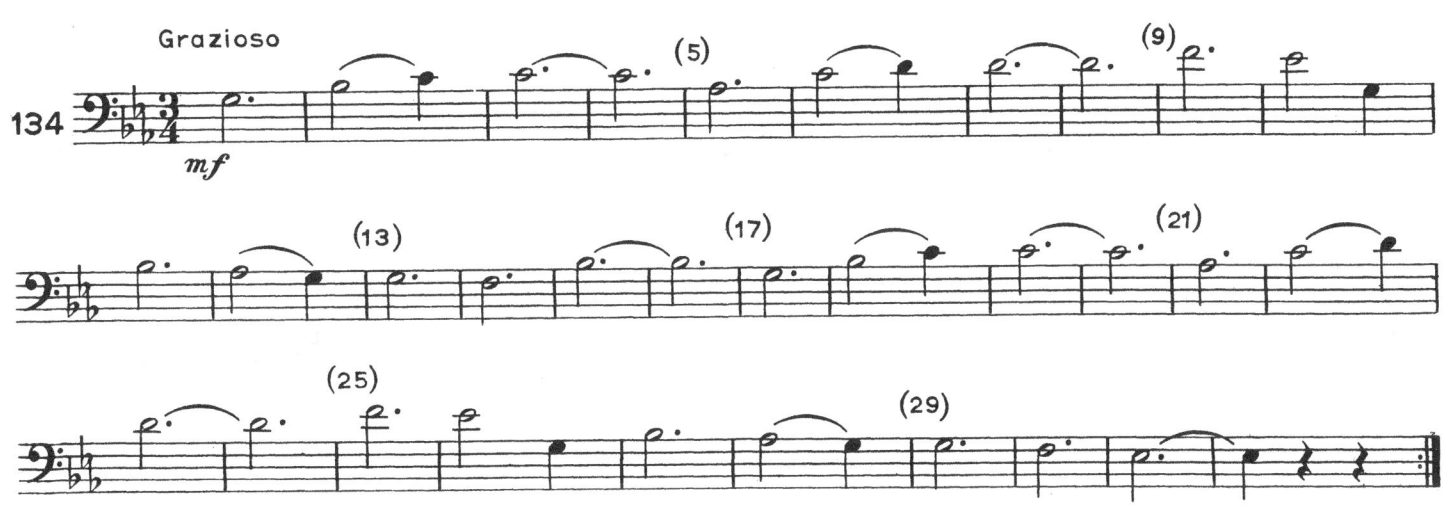

Swanee River
STEPHEN C. FOSTER

Key of A Major

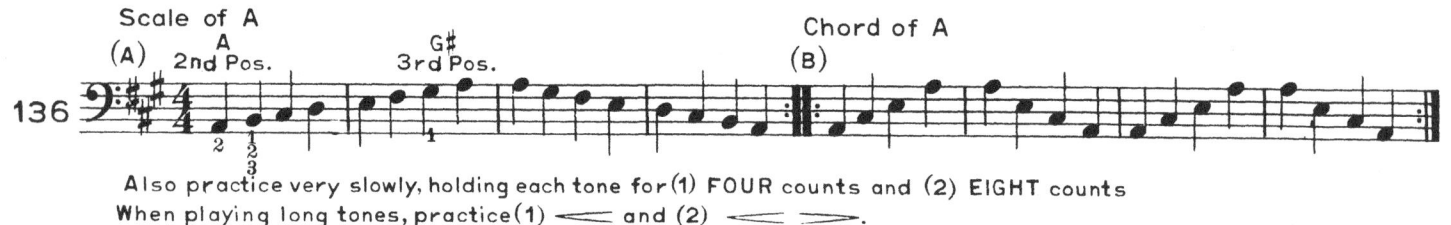

Also practice very slowly, holding each tone for (1) FOUR counts and (2) EIGHT counts
When playing long tones, practice (1) < and (2) < >.

SLURS

Also practice very slowly, holding each tone of each slur for FOUR counts.

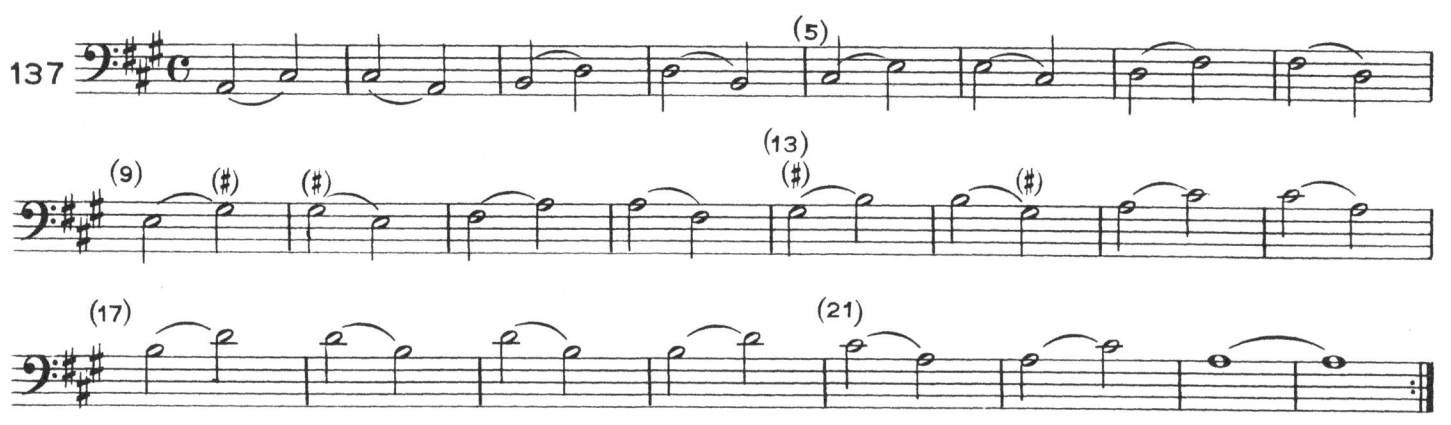

SHORT EXERCISES EMPLOYING "G#"

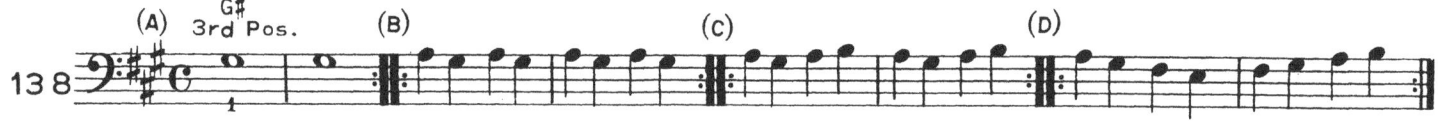

AURA LEE

Old Song

EXCERPT from L'ARLESIENNE SUITE

BIZET

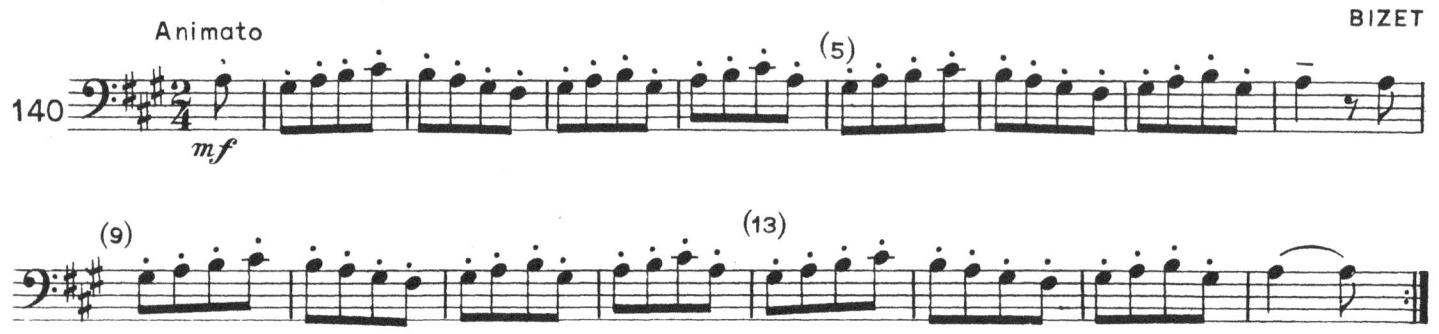

AMERICAN PIONEER SONG
Traditional

DEVELOPING "LOW B♮"

This tone usually is too sharp. Flatten the pitch sufficiently to produce it well in tune.

DEVELOPING "LOW A"

SHORT EXERCISES EMPLOYING "LOW B" and "LOW A"

MELODY IN THE LOW RANGE
W.B. BRADBURY

Key of A♭ Major

Also practice very slowly, holding each tone for (1) FOUR counts and (2) EIGHT counts.

When playing long tones, practice (1) ─< and (2) ─<─>.

SLURS

Also practice very slowly, holding each tone of each slur for FOUR counts.

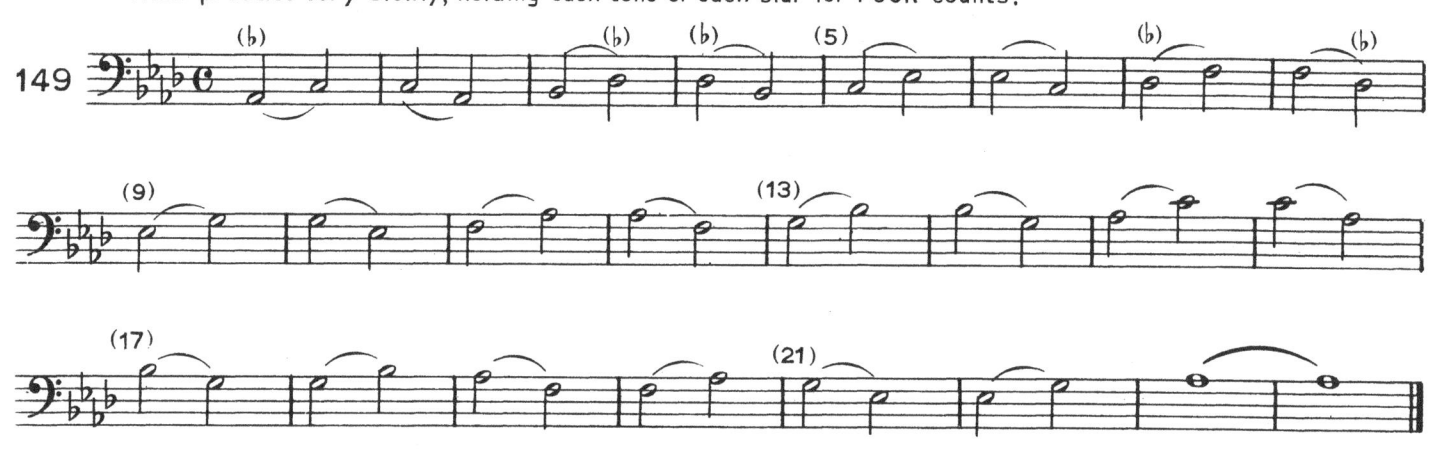

INTRODUCING "HIGH D♭"

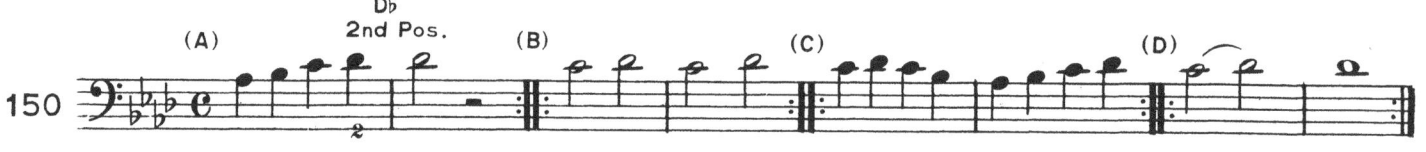

SPRING SONG

FERRERA

* *D.C.* = Go back to the beginning.   *Fine* = end

Key of D♭ Major

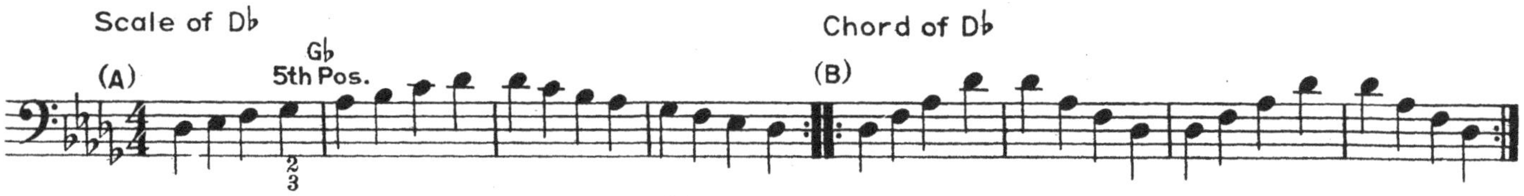

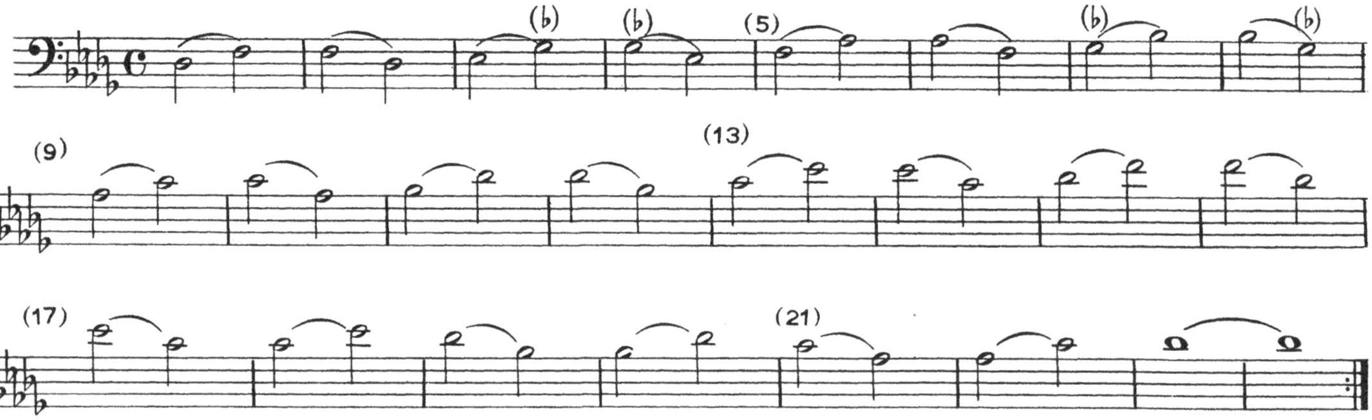

THE FIRST NOEL

OLD WELSH MELODY
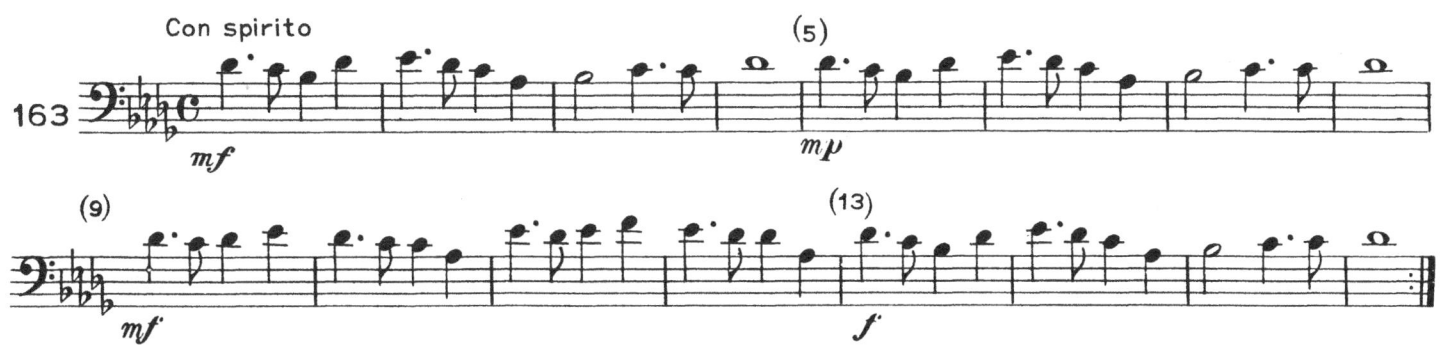

Barcarolle from Tales of Hoffmann
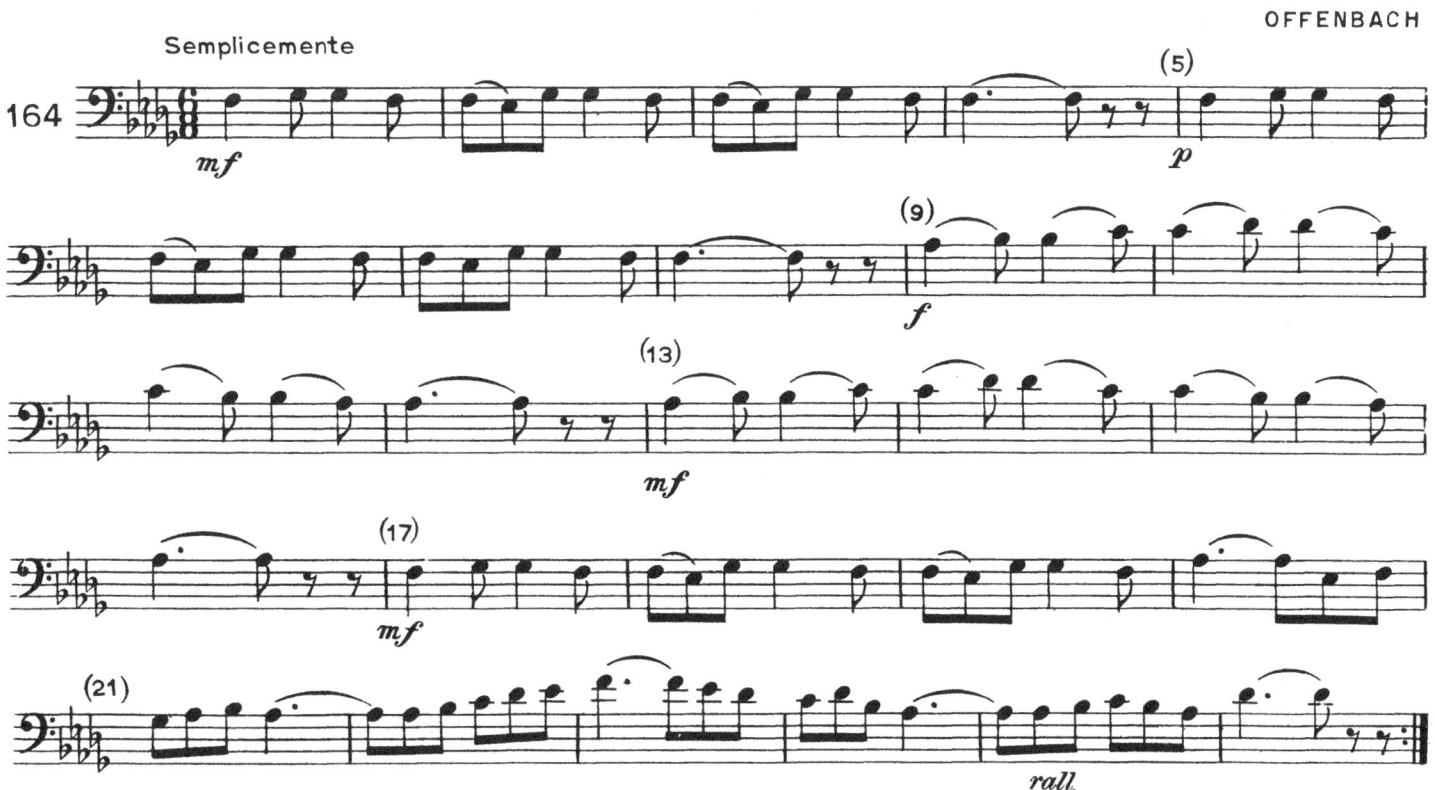

Developing Low Tones

Chromatic Scales

Also practice very slowly, holding each tone for EIGHT counts.
When playing long tones, practice (1) $<$ and (2) $<\!\!>$.

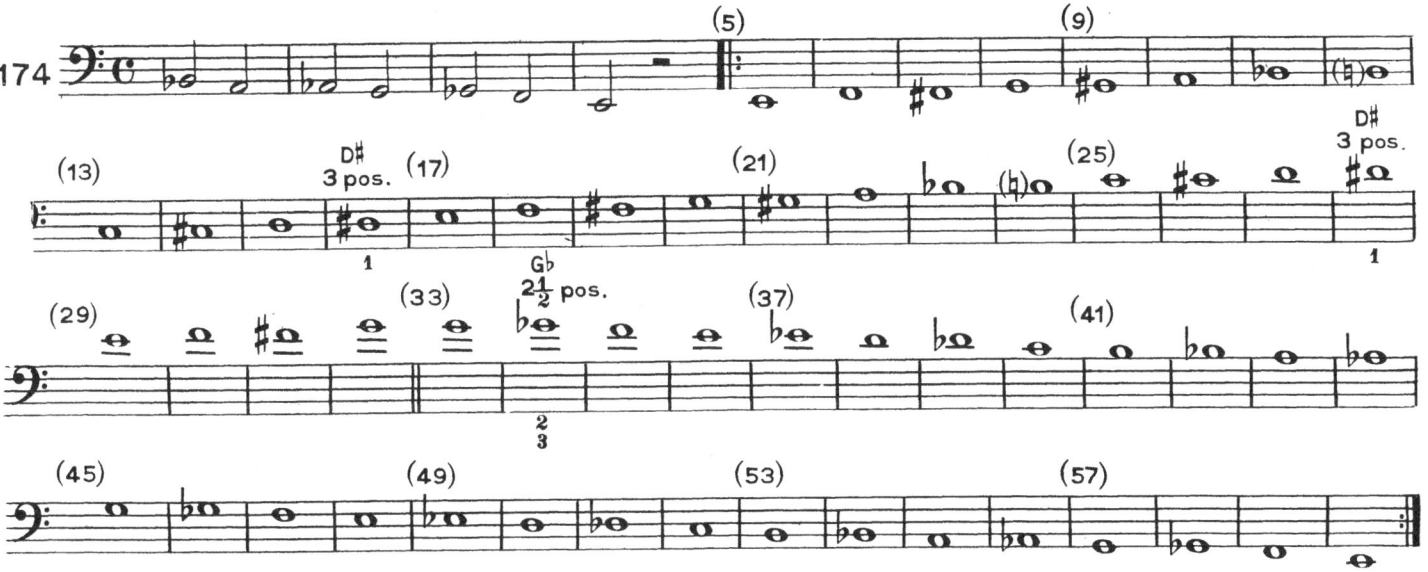

SHORT CHROMATIC STUDIES

Also practice very slowly, holding each tone for (1) FOUR counts and (2) EIGHT counts.
When playing long tones, practice (1) $<$ and (2) $<\!\!>$.
Also practice very legato, (1) slurring each two tones, and (2) slurring each four tones.

Arban Foundation Studies

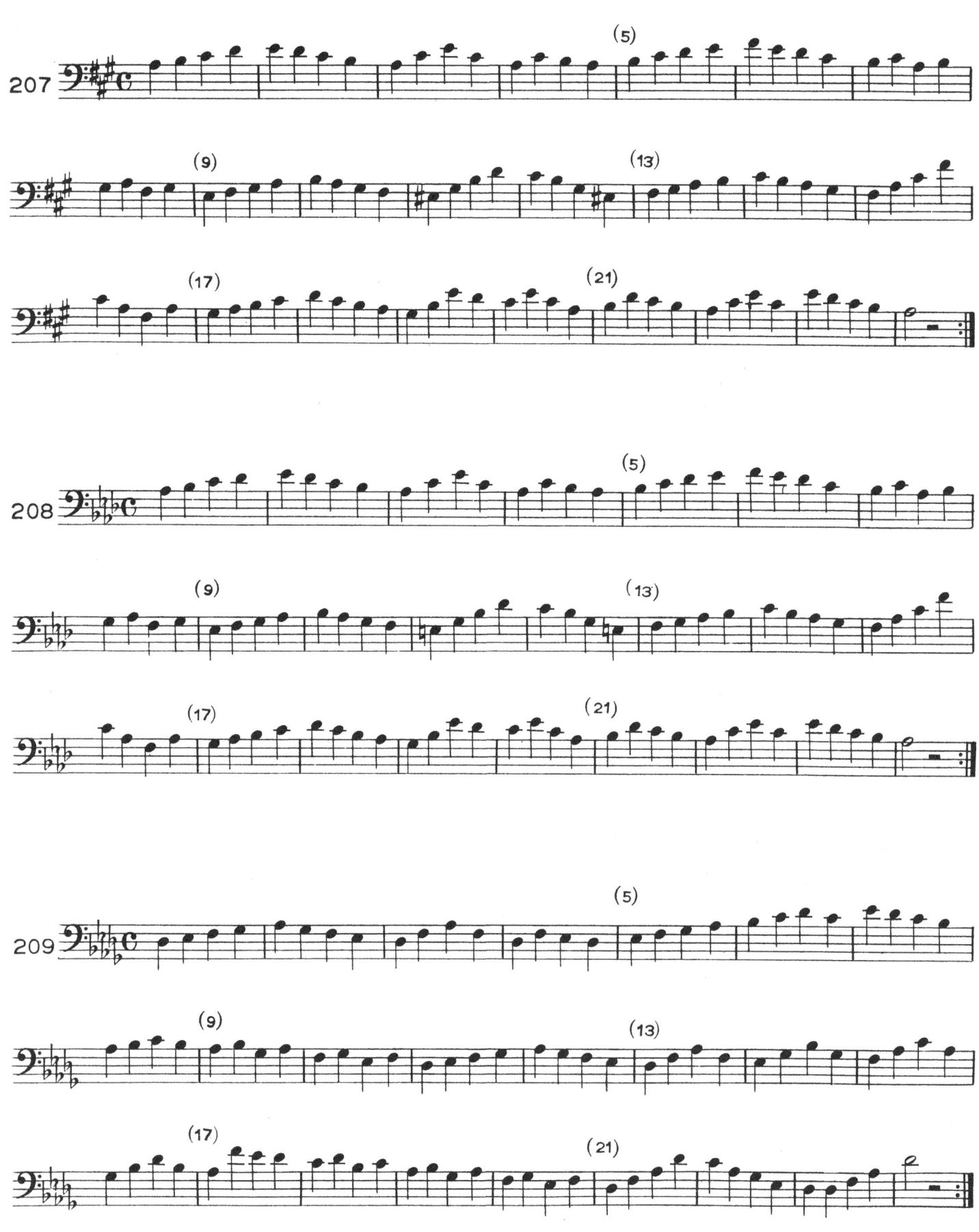

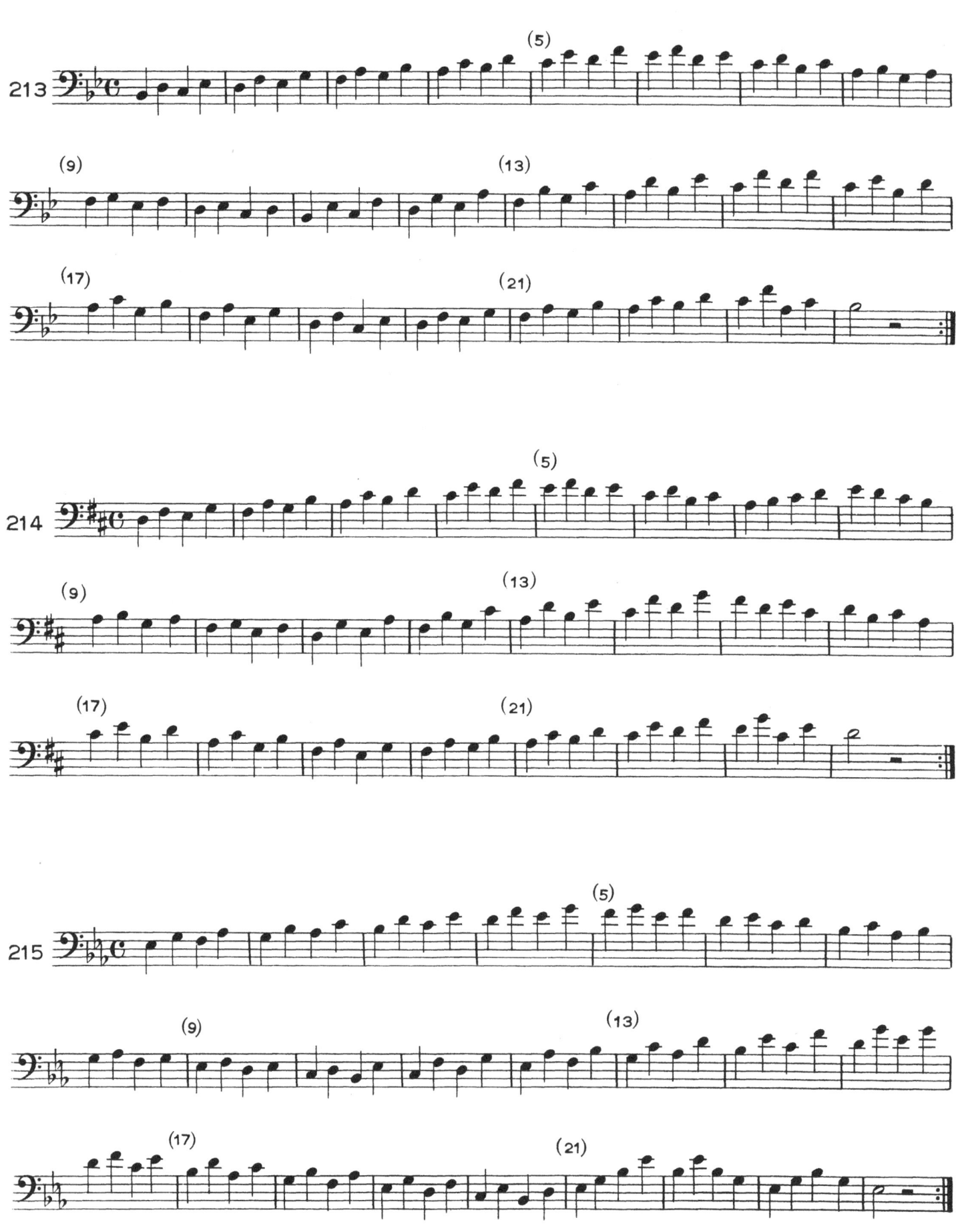

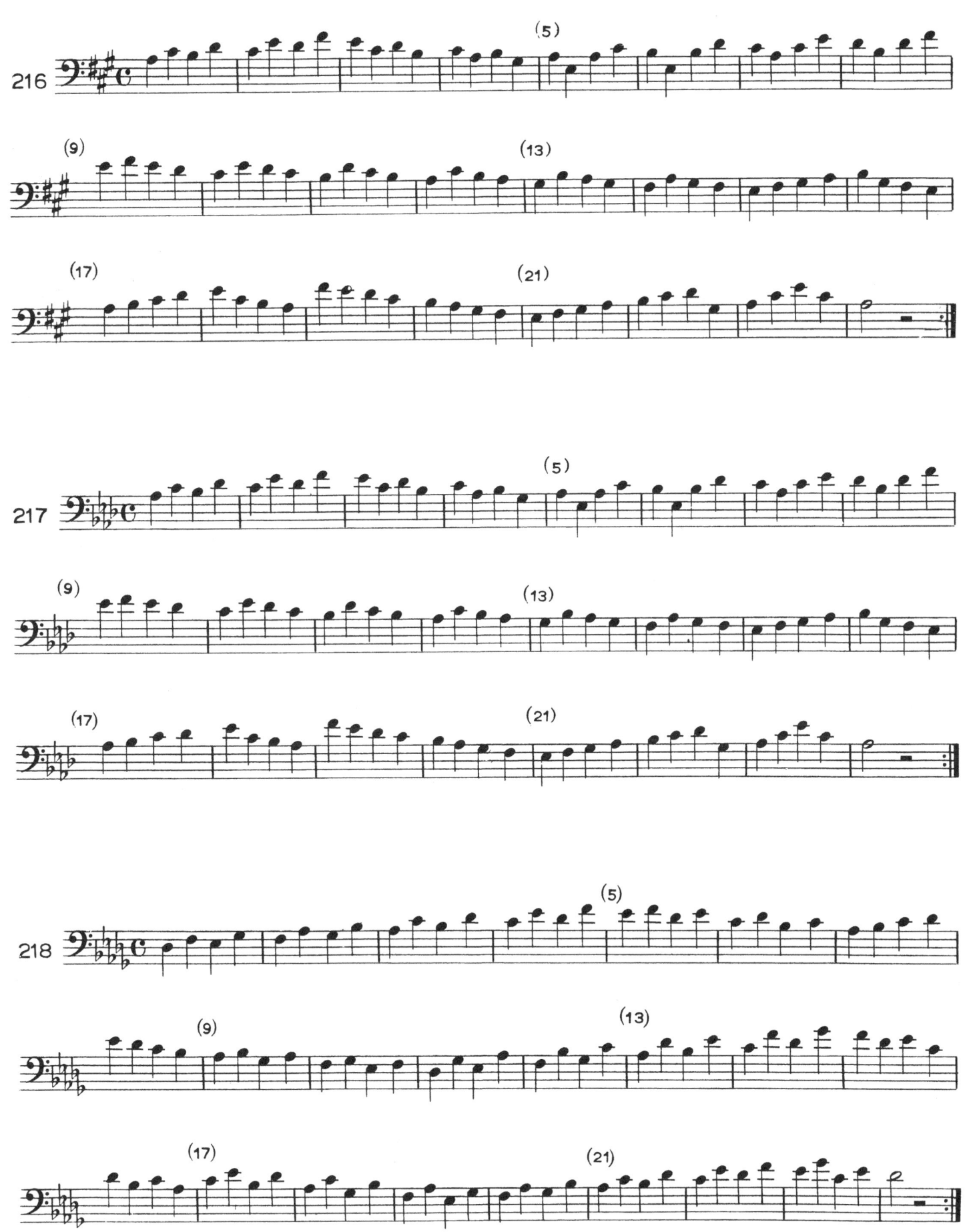

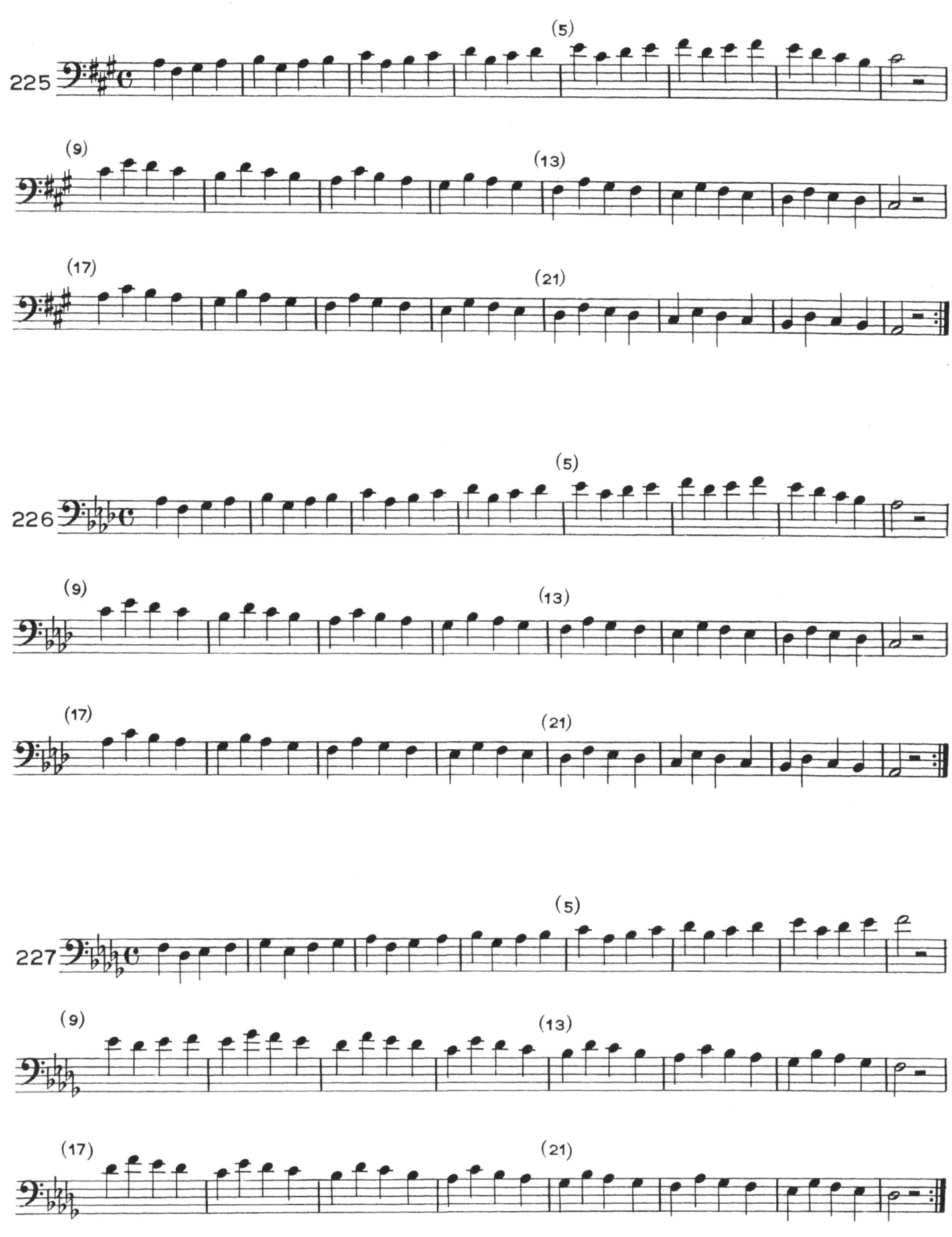

Arban Interval Slurs

(a) Also practice very slowly, holding each tone of each slur for FOUR counts.
(b) Also practice tonguing each note.

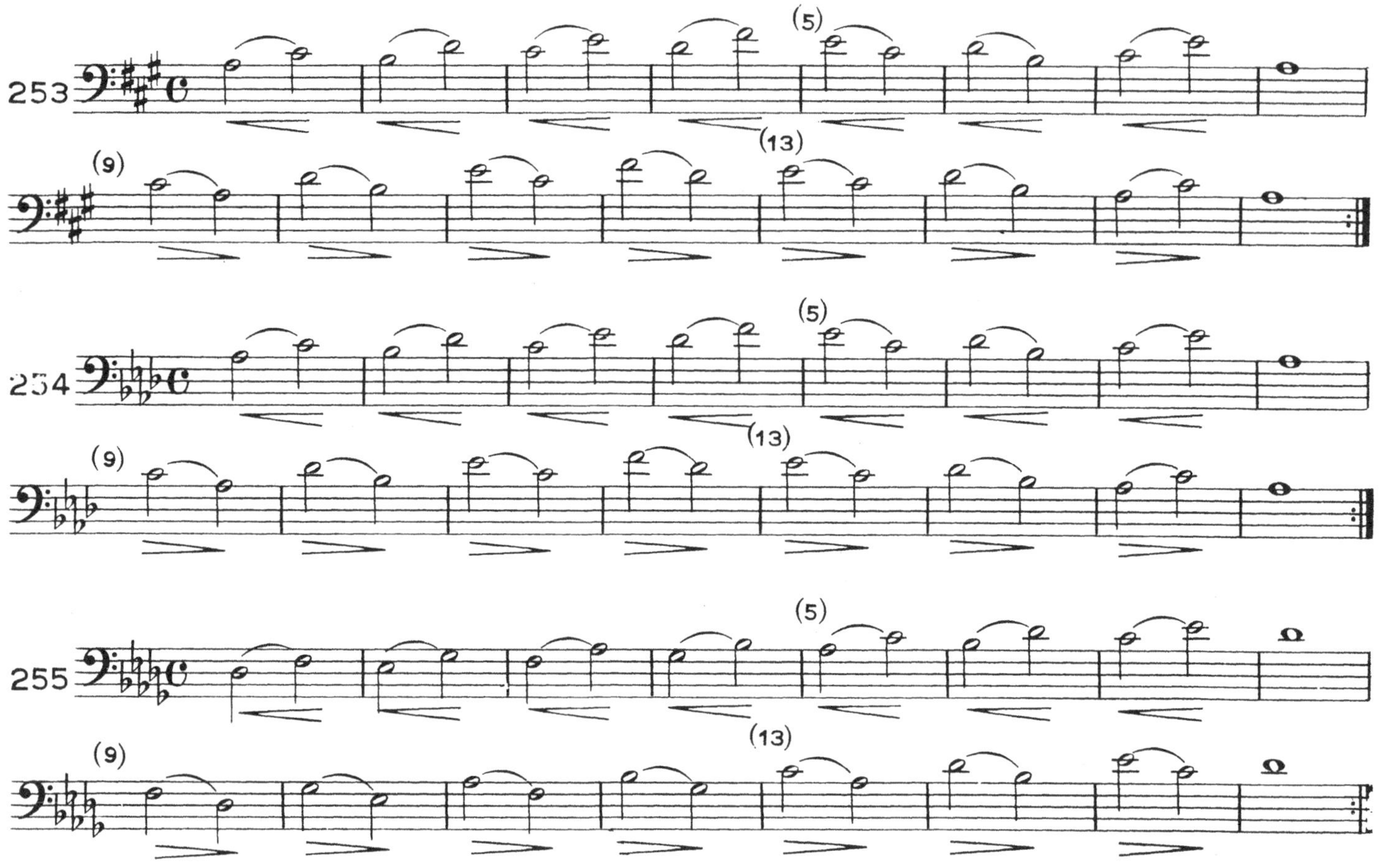

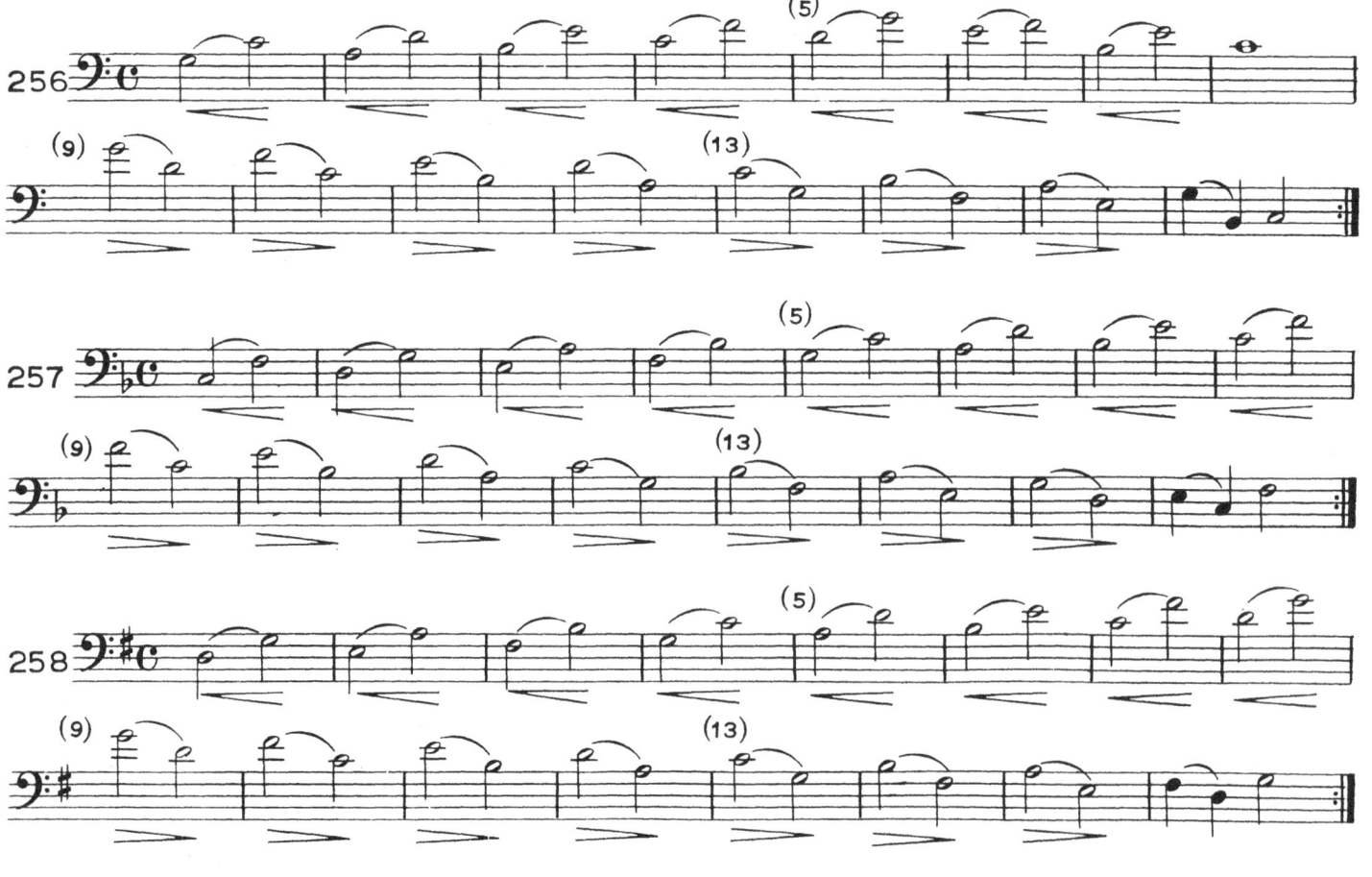

Arban Lip Slurs

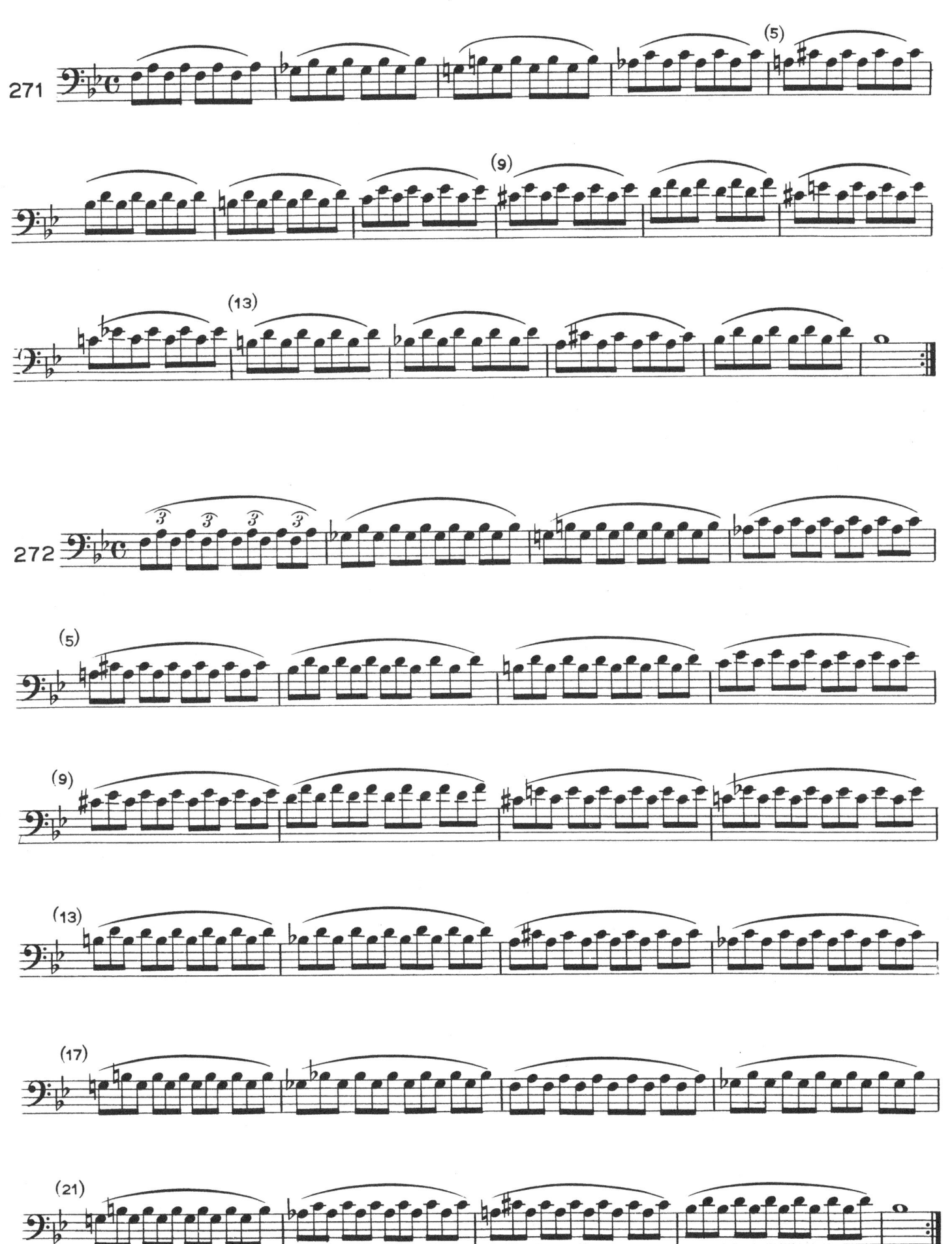

Rhythmic Studies and Excerpts

Selected from the works of ARBAN, ST. JACOME and others

INTRODUCING SIXTEENTH NOTES

273
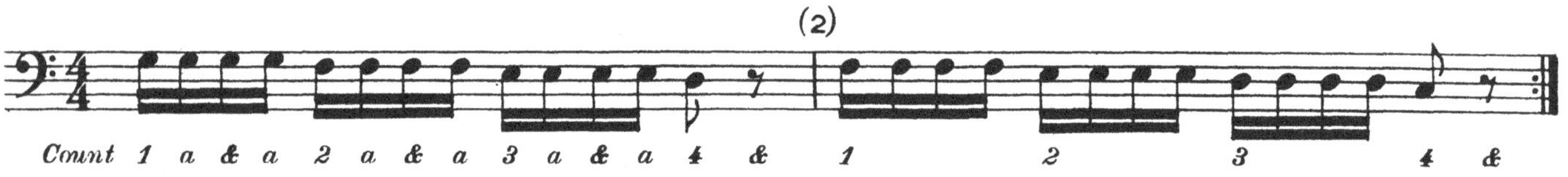
(2)
Count 1 a & a 2 a & a 3 a & a 4 & 1 2 3 4 &

QUARTER AND SIXTEENTH NOTES ALTERNATED

274
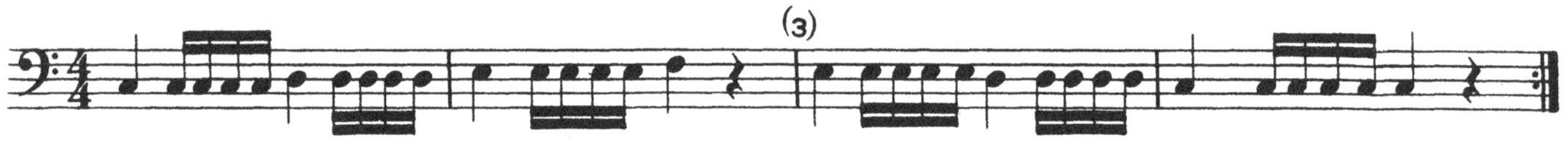
(3)

FIERCE FLAMES ARE RAGING

from Il Trovatore

VERDI

275
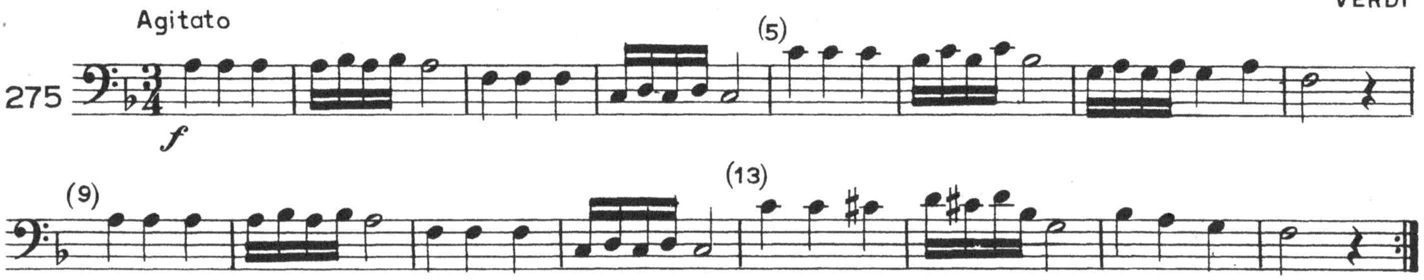
Agitato
f
(5)
(9)
(13)

RHYTHMICAL STUDY

276
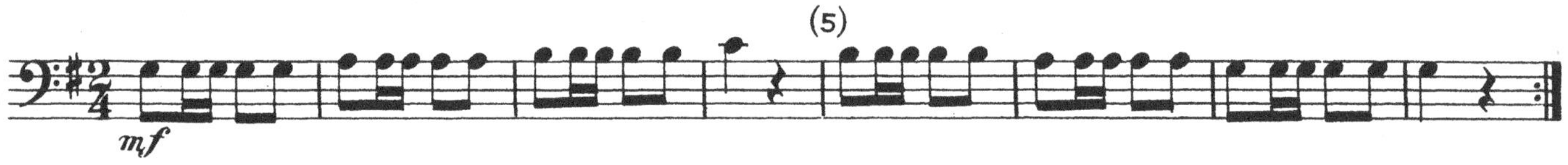
mf
(5)

ARBAN STUDY

277
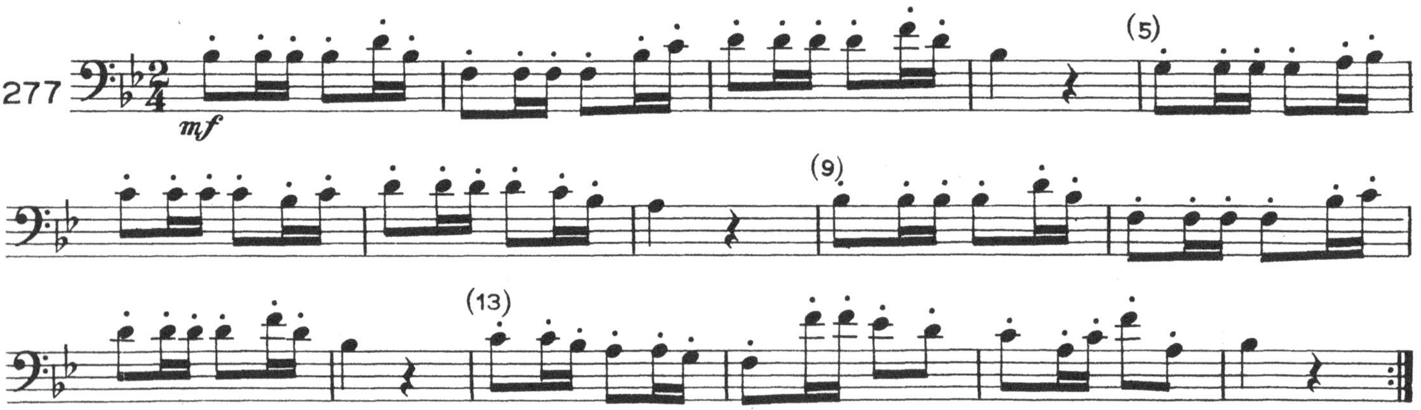
mf
(5)
(9)
(13)

FANFARE

278
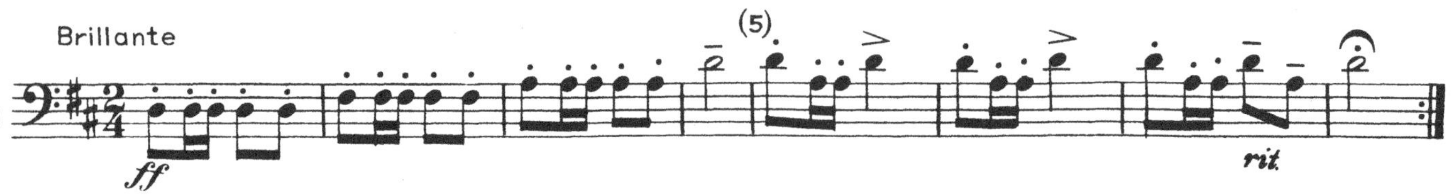
Brillante
ff
(5)
rit.

TRIPLETS

QUARTER NOTES AND TRIPLETS ALTERNATED

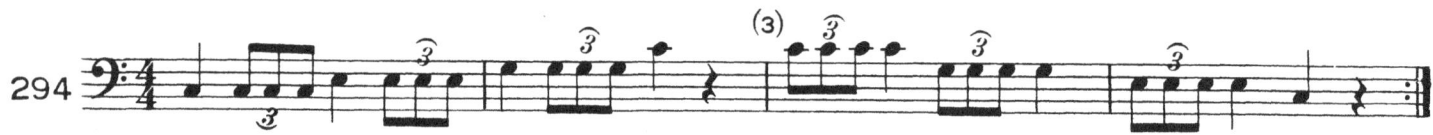

PILGRIMS' CHORUS
from Tannhaüser
WAGNER

ANDANTE
from Fifth Symphony
TSCHAIKOWSKY

SOLDIERS' CHORUS
from Faust
GOUNOD

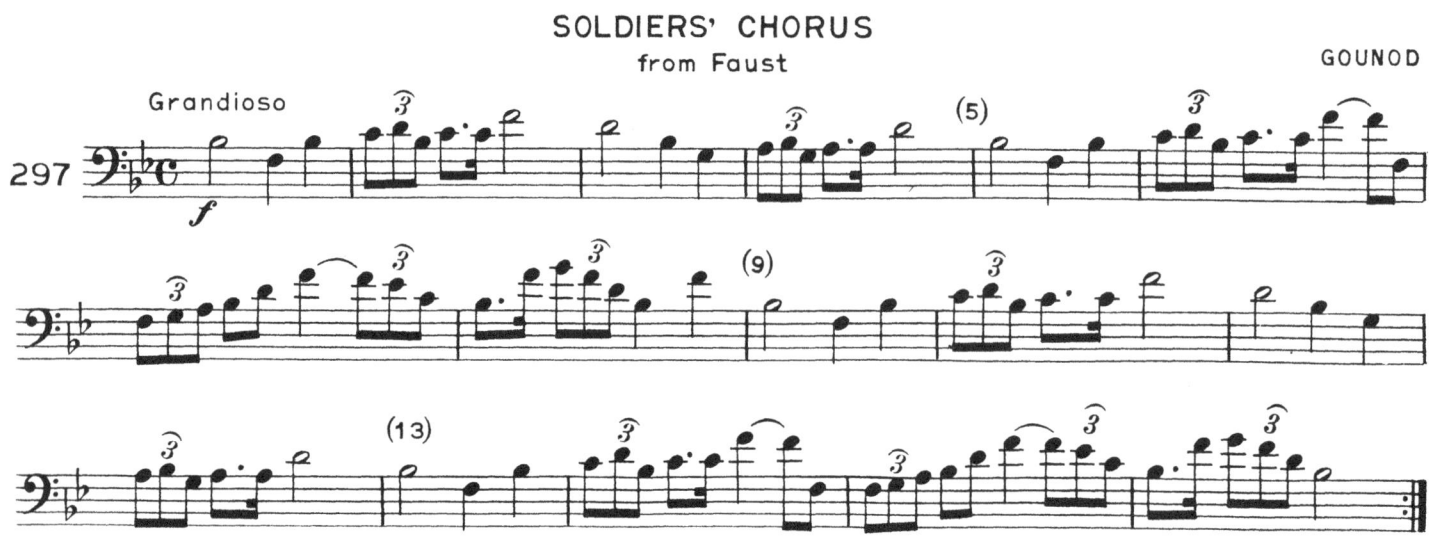

INTRODUCING SYNCOPATION

FINALE, Second Act of ZAMPA
HEROLD

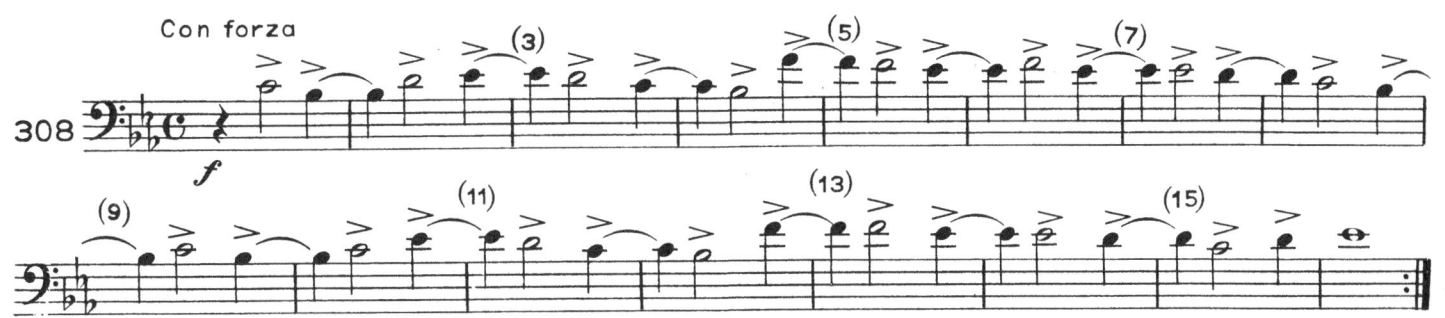

THE SIXTEENTH NOTE FOLLOWED BY A DOTTED EIGHTH NOTE

SWING LOW, SWEET CHARIOT
HARRY T. BURLEIGH

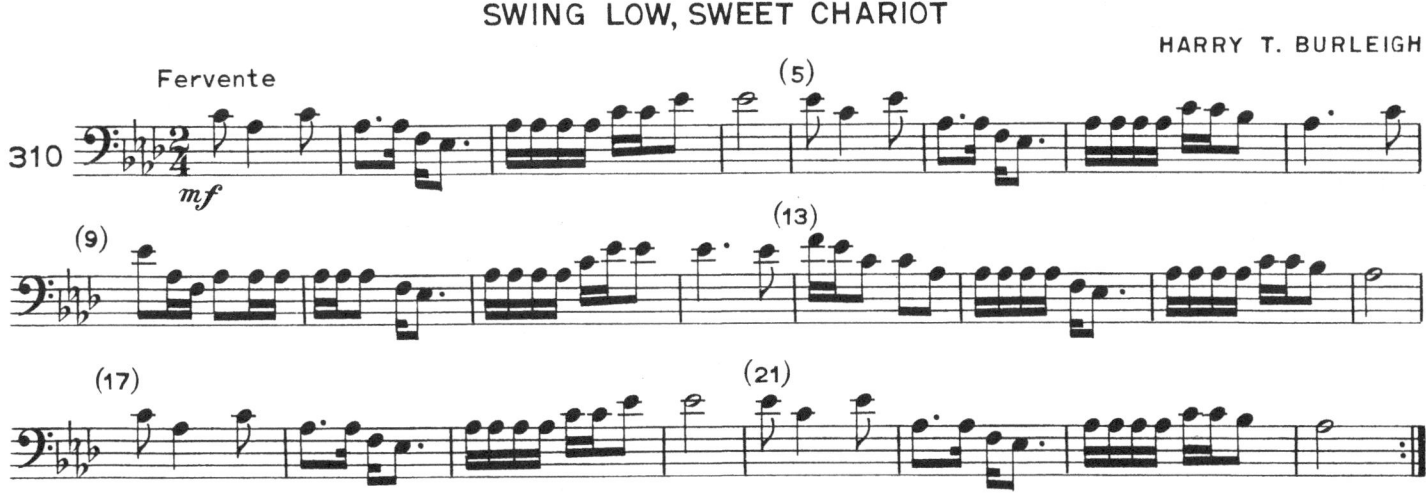

TANGO
ALBENIZ

At this stage of advancement the student, in addition to continuing his study of Modern Arban-St.Jacome in a systematic fashion, should turn to MODERN PARES FOUNDATION STUDIES FOR TROMBONE OR BARITONE (published by Rubank,Inc.) a companion volume to the present work, and begin at once the all important procedure of daily scale practice.

St. Jacome Articulation Studies

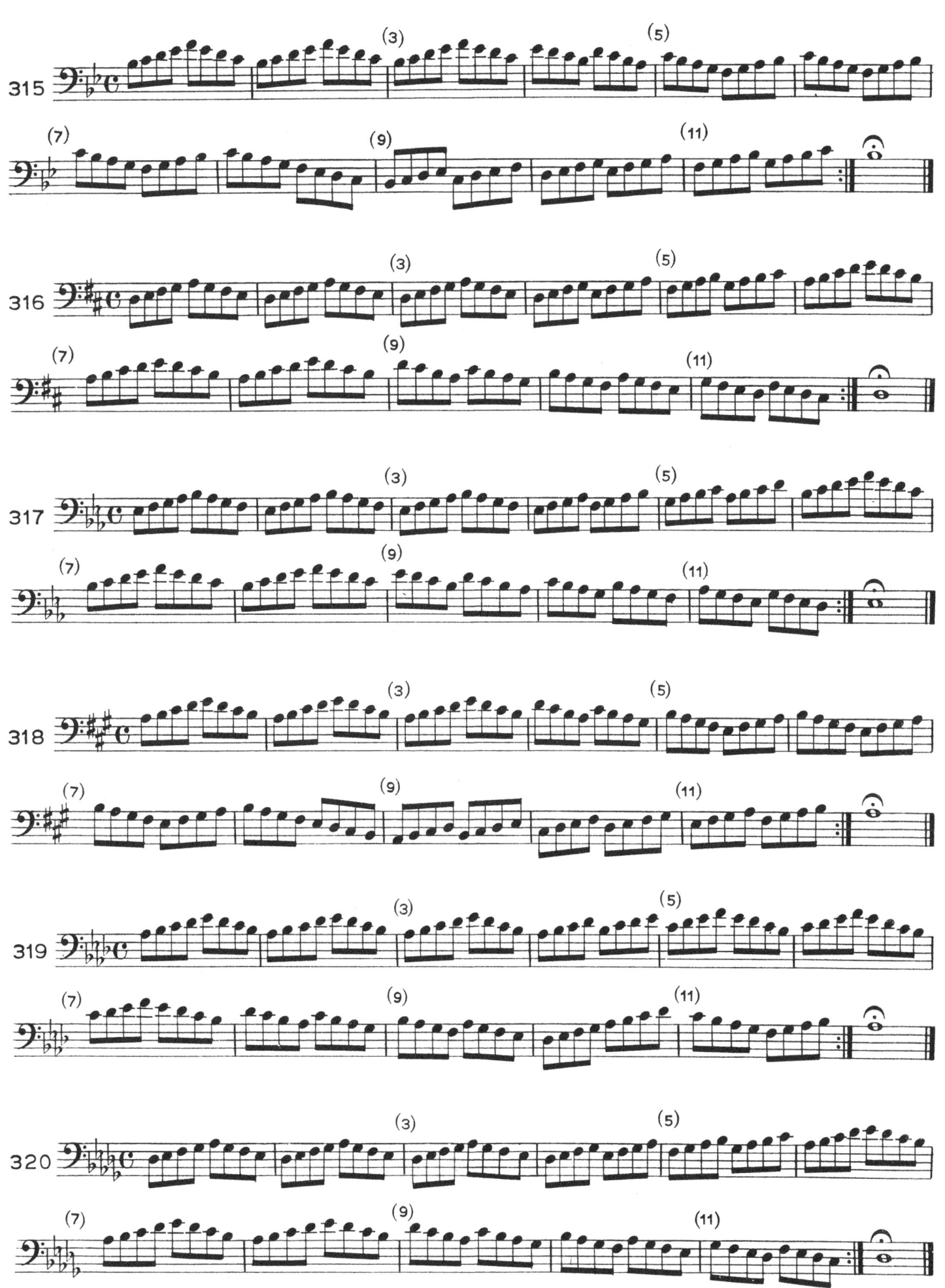

St. Jacome Lip Exercises

TROMBONE = FIRST POSITION   BARITONE = OPEN TONE

321 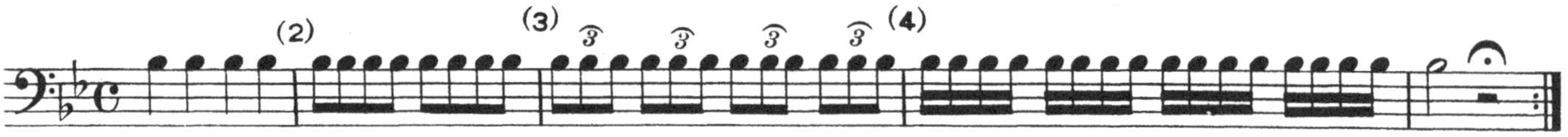

322 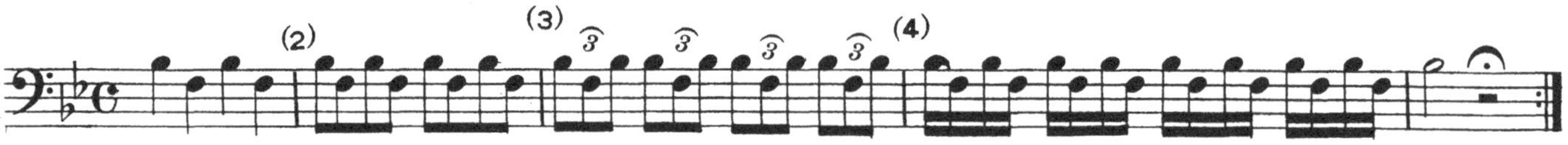

323 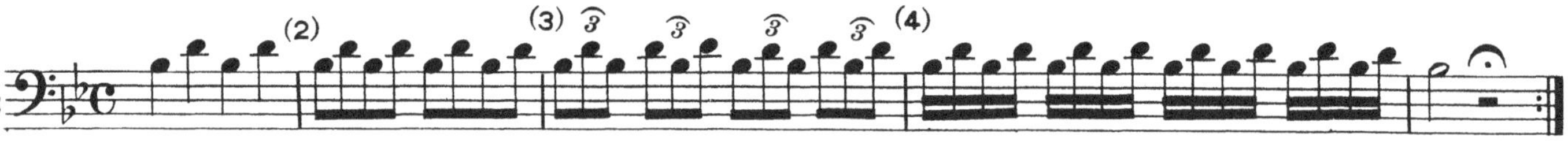

324 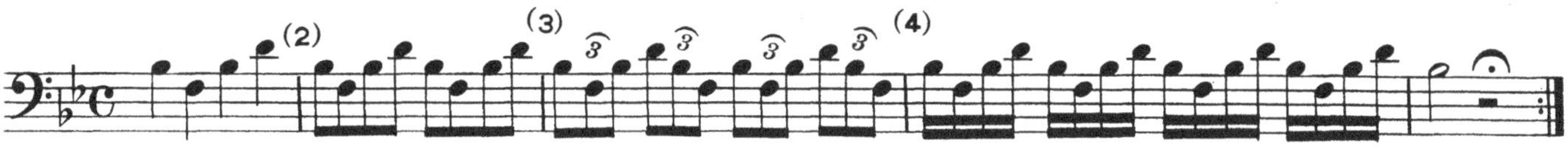

325 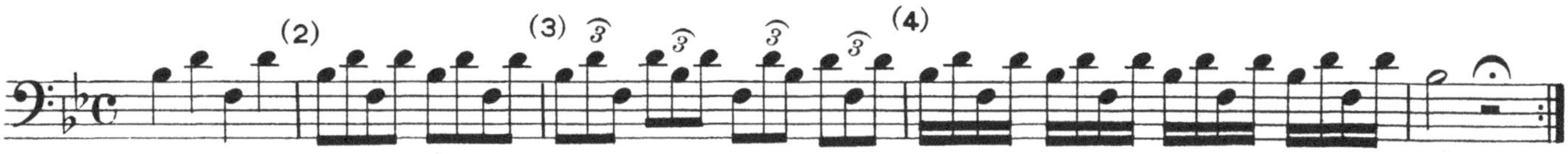

326 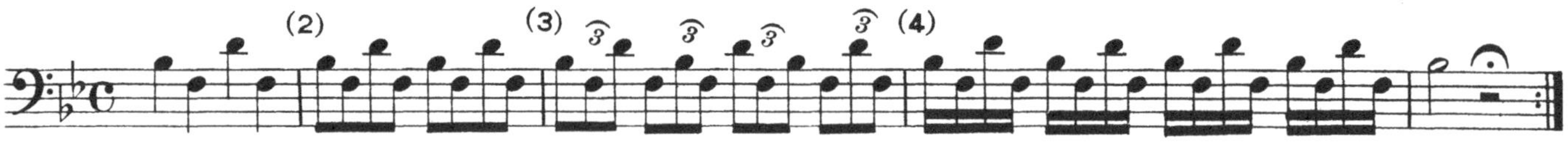

TROMBONE = THIRD POSITION   BARITONE = FIRST VALVE

327

328

329

330

331

332

1008-103

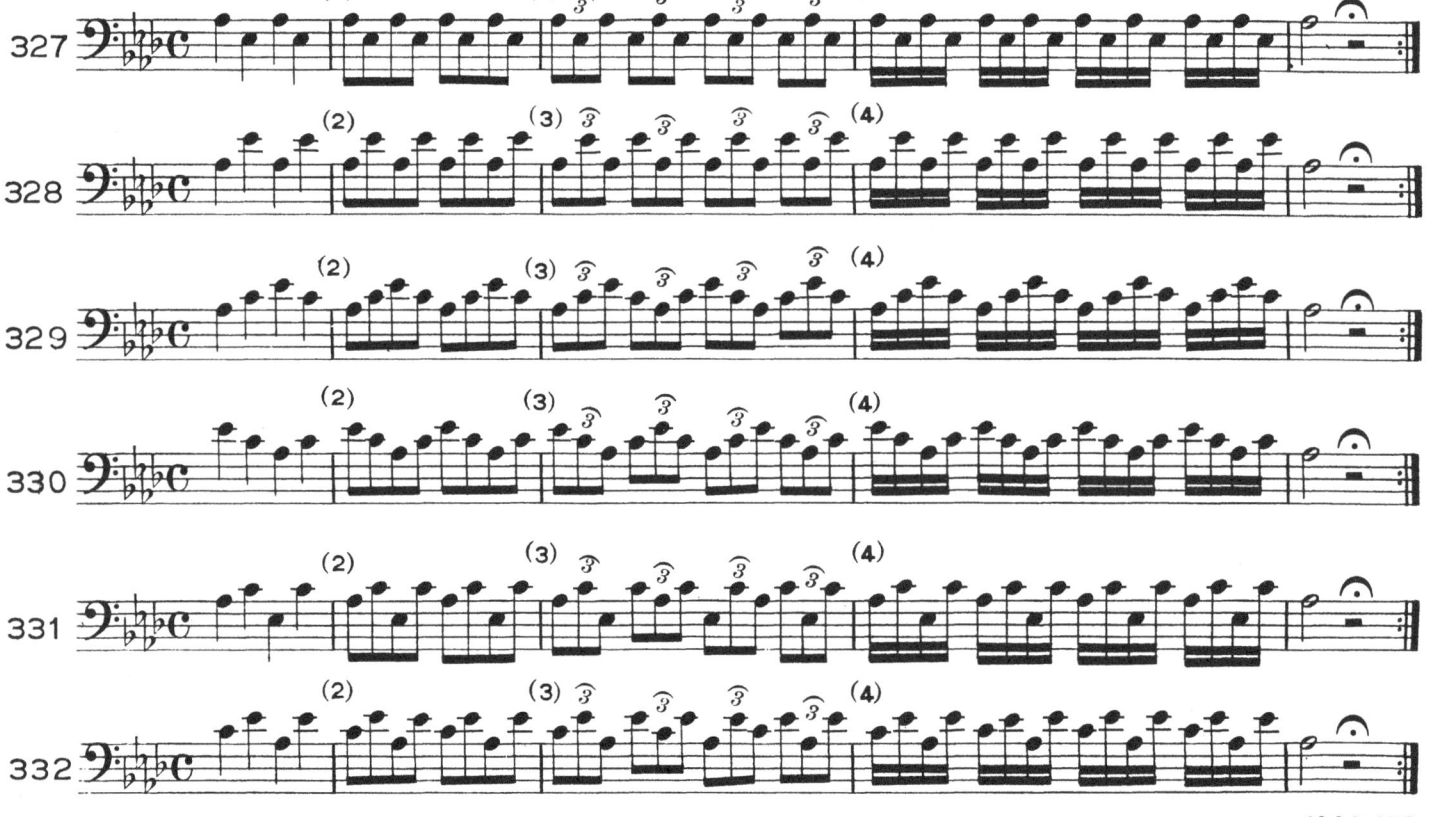

Major Scales in Thirds

Basic Lip Slurs

Introducing Alla Breve (Cut) Time

Alla Breve (Cut) Time is 4/4 Time (Meter) with TWO BEATS to the measure instead of four. It is indicated by the sign ¢

Trombone or Baritone Duets

Selected from the works of ARBAN, ST. JACOME, CARNAUD and others.

FIRST DUET IN COMMON OR ALLA BREVE TIME

(Before playing duets in Alla Breve Time, carefully study this procedure as illustrated on page 70.)

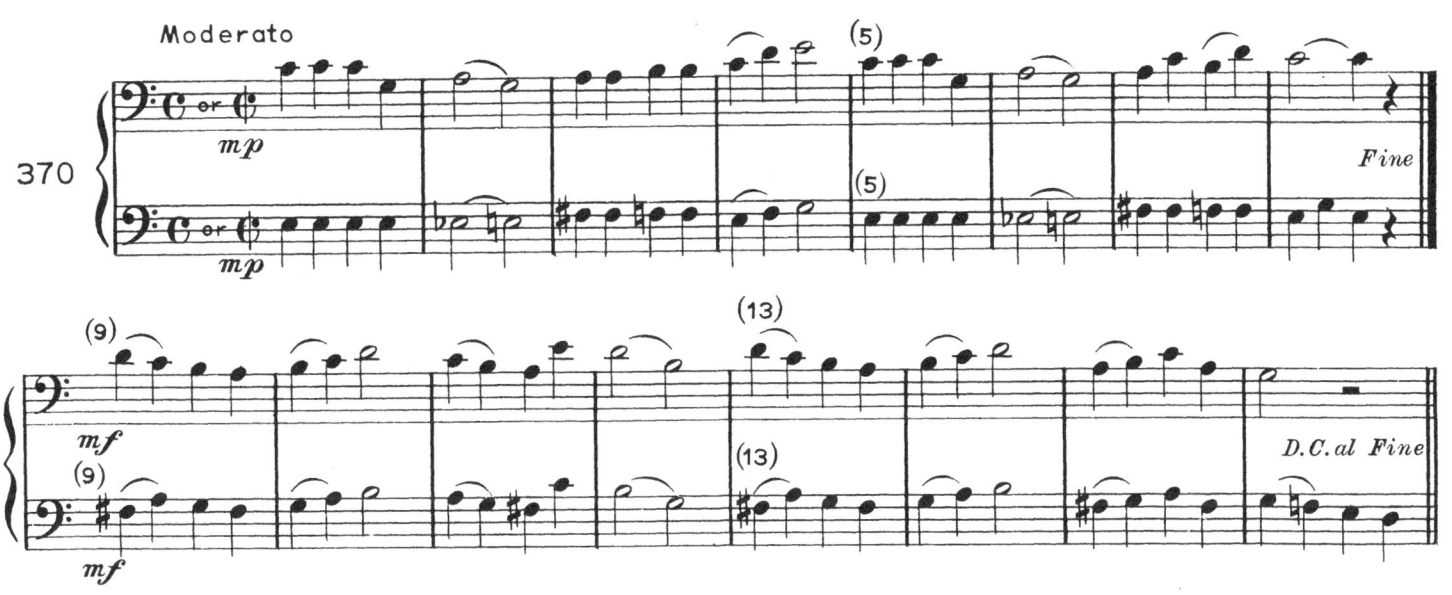

SCOTCH AIR

Traditional

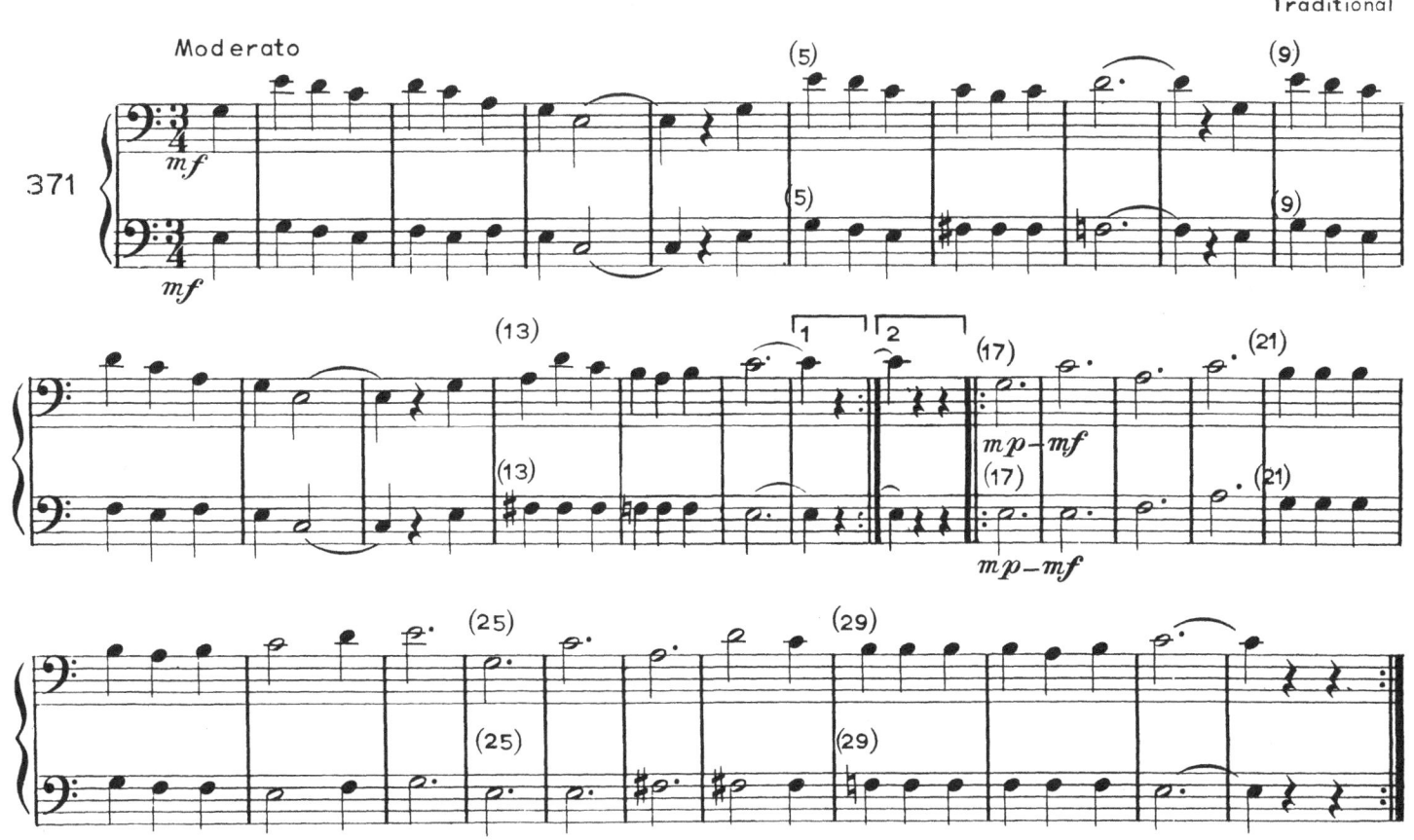

SECOND DUET IN COMMON OR ALLA BREVE TIME

WALTZ IN DUET STYLE

von BLON

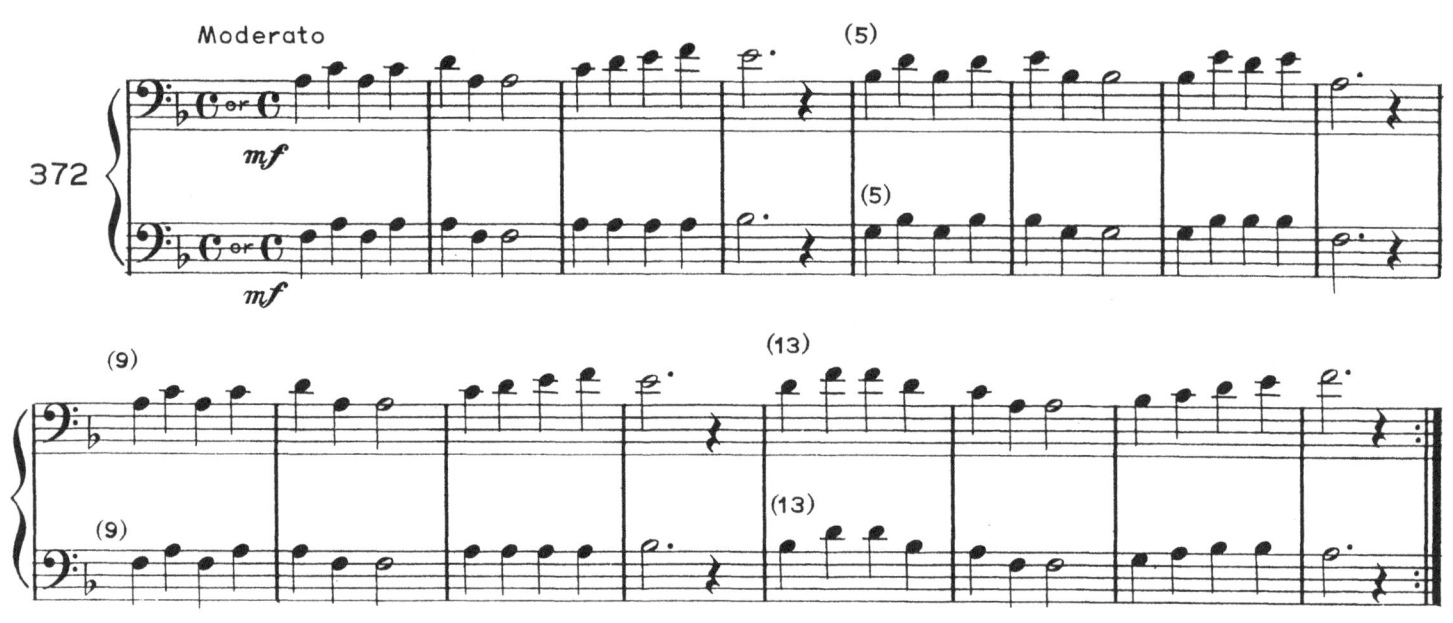

THIRD DUET IN COMMON OR ALLA BREVE TIME

CARNAUD

Moderato

374

Old Black Joe

STEPHEN C. FOSTER

Affetuosamente

375

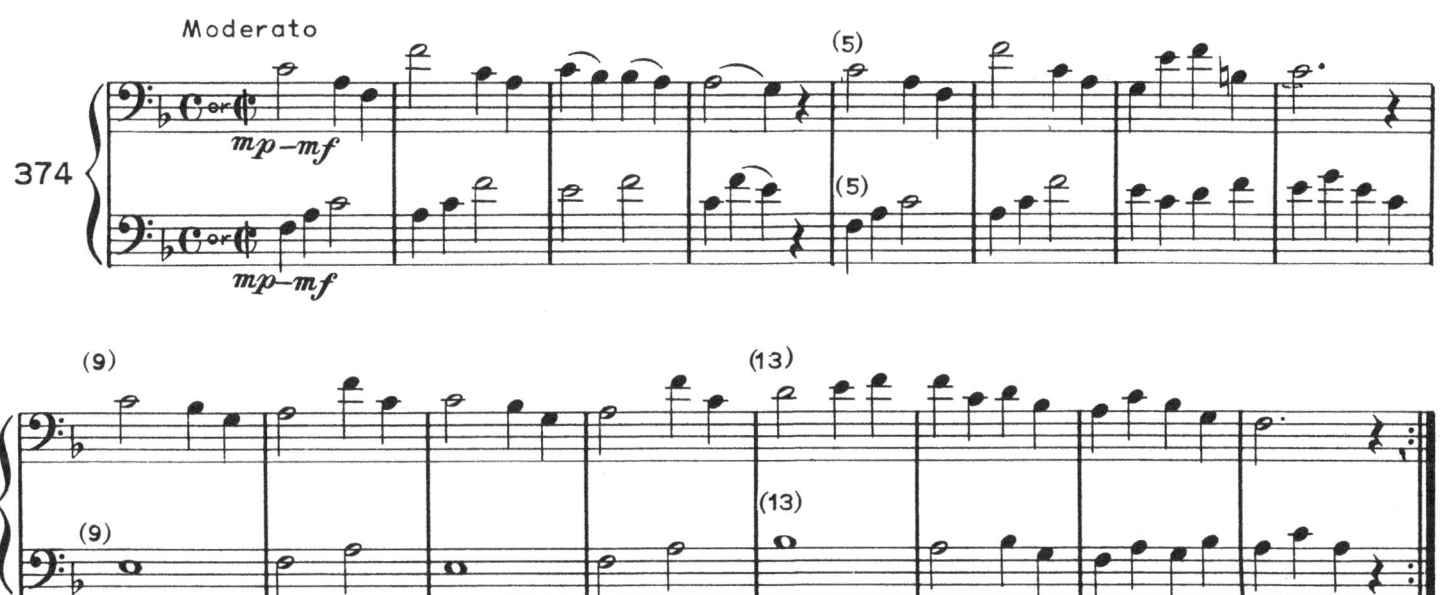

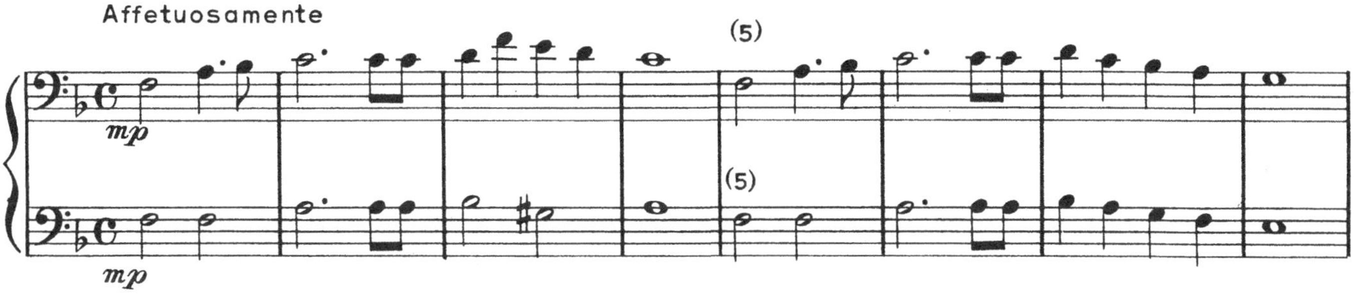

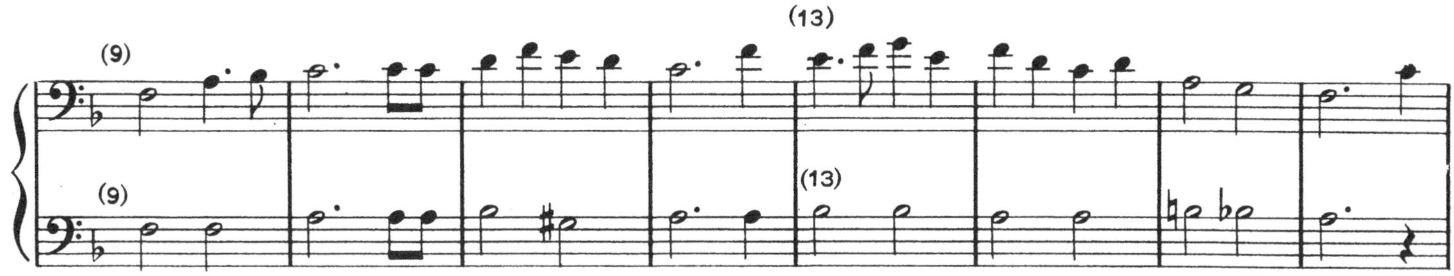

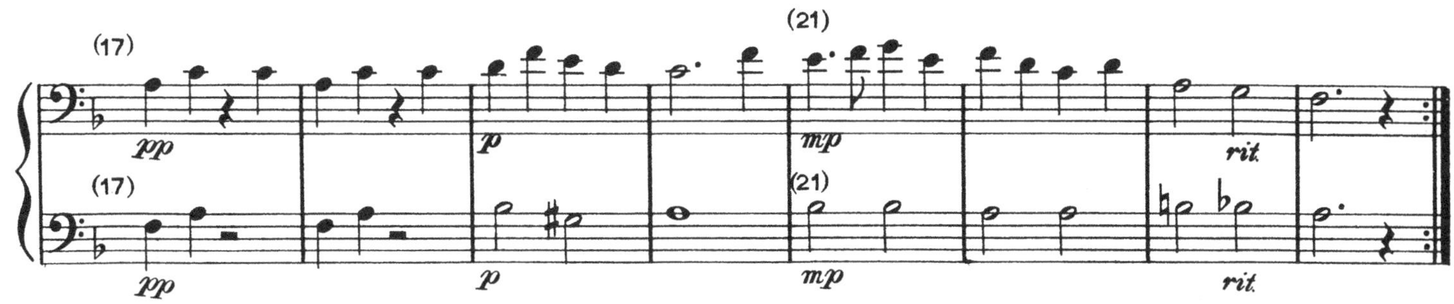

TRADITIONAL DUET IN COMMON OR ALLA BREVE TIME

ST. JACOME

Londonderry Air

Traditional

RHYTHMICAL DUET IN COMMON OR ALLA BREVE TIME

ST. JACOME

Viennese Melody

Traditional

Just A Song at Twilight

MOLLOY

380

Auld Lang Syne

Scottish Folk Song

381

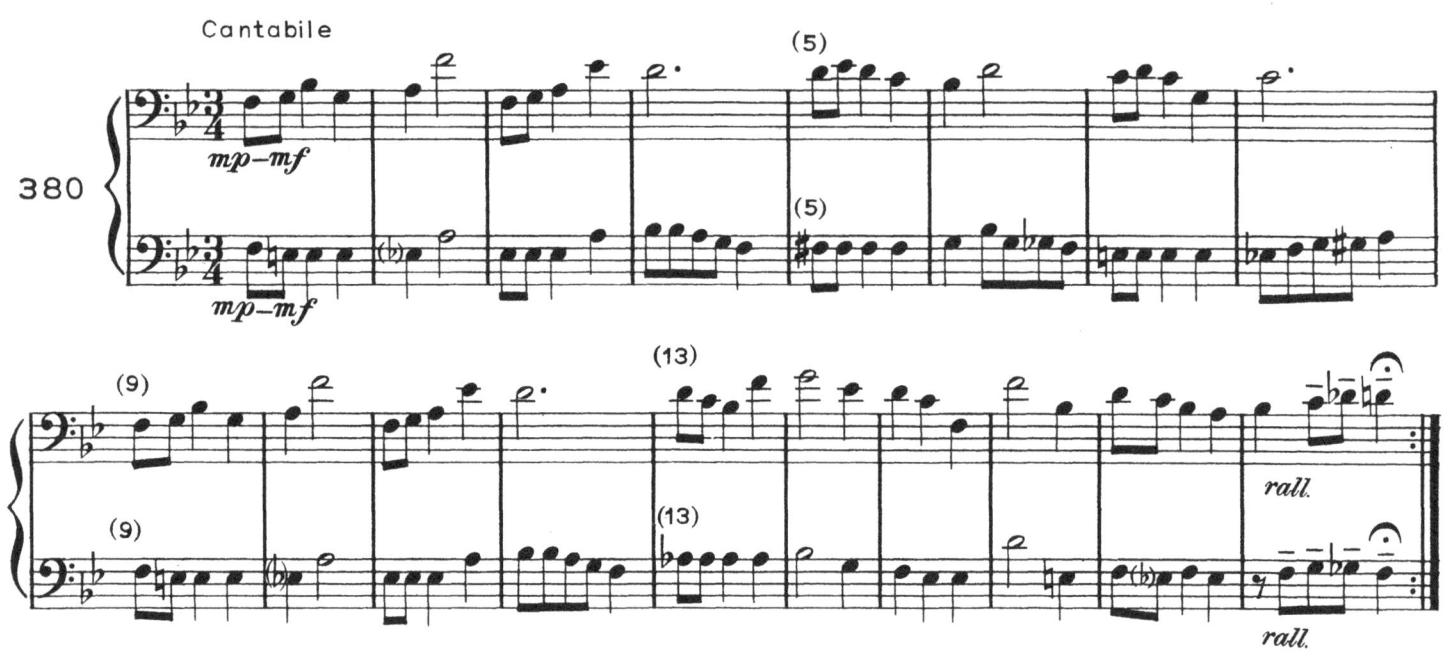

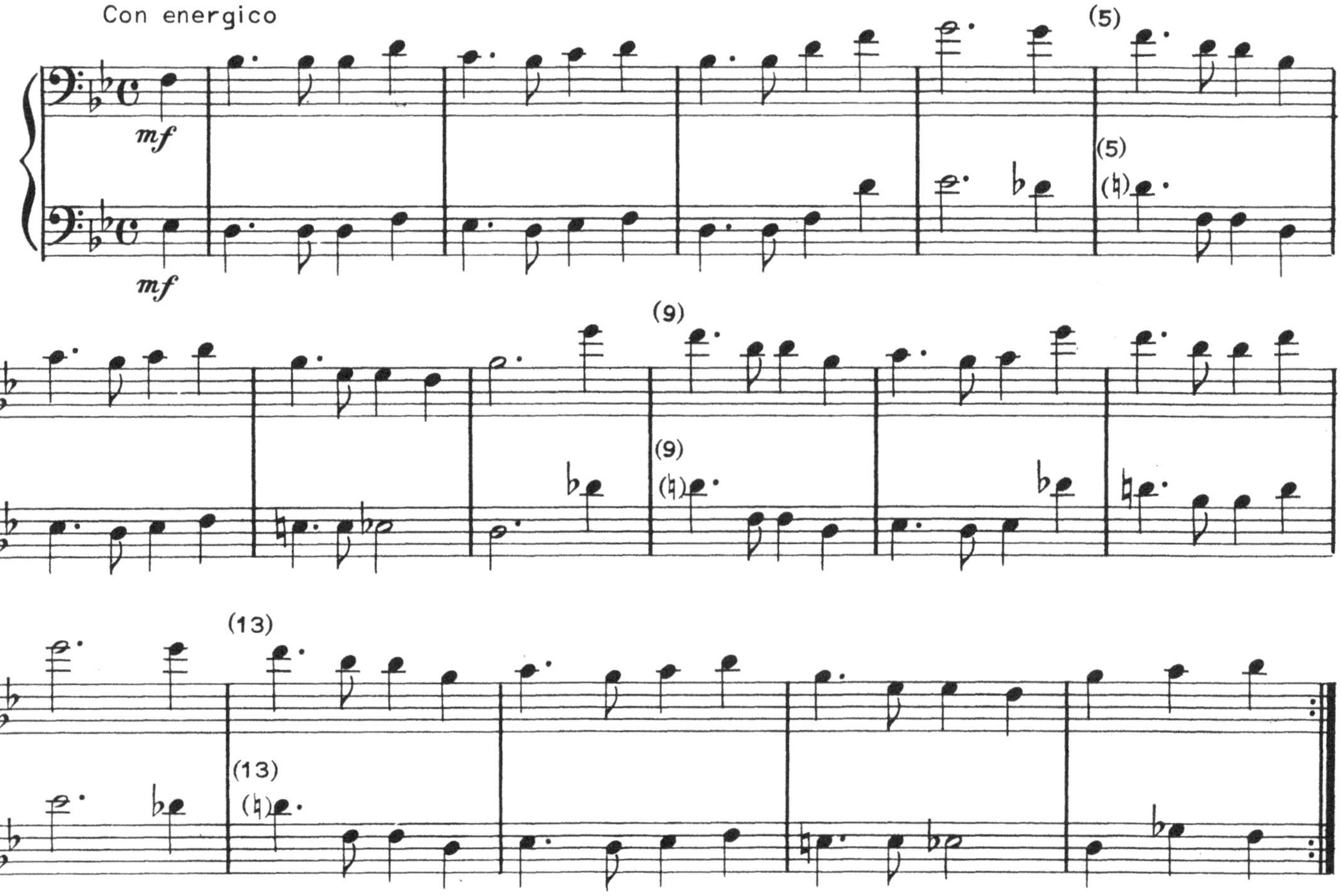

Rondo

CARNAUD

Romance

REDOWA

L'Elisire D'Amore

DONIZETTI

THEME
BEETHOVEN

Carry Me Back to Old Virginny
JAMES A. BLAND

Allegro de Concert No.1

ST. JACOME

387

Allegro de Concert No. 2

ST. JACOME

Musical Embellishments (Ornamentation)

The Modern Grace Note (known theoretically as an ACCIACCATURA) is a small ornamental note written with a line through its stem. It is played quickly and its time value is taken from that of the note preceding it rather than from that of the note to which it is attached.

SINGLE GRACE NOTES

ARBAN

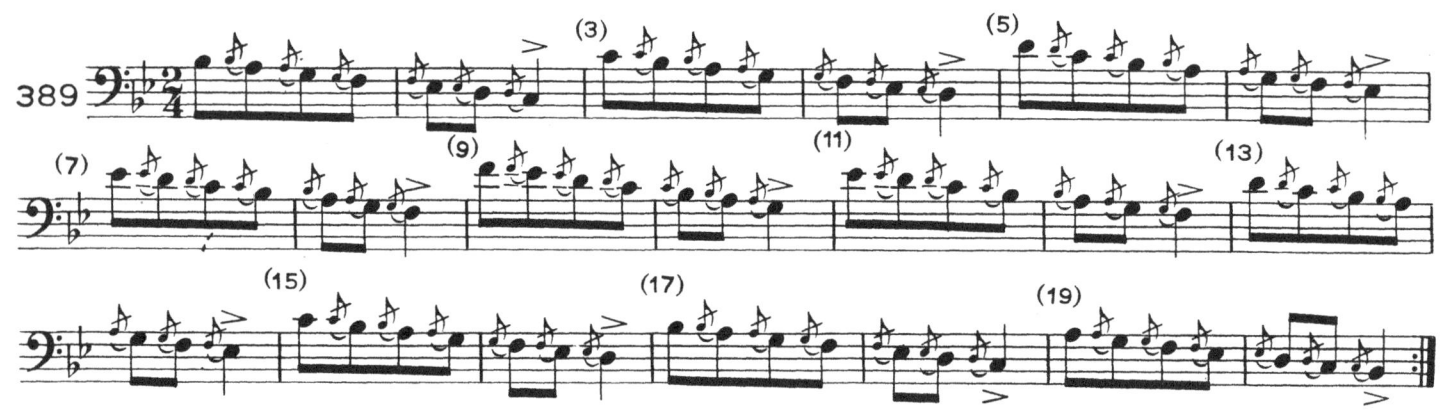

DOUBLE GRACE NOTES

ST. JACOME

TRIPLE GRACE NOTES

Slurring indicated below notes is for baritone only.

ARBAN

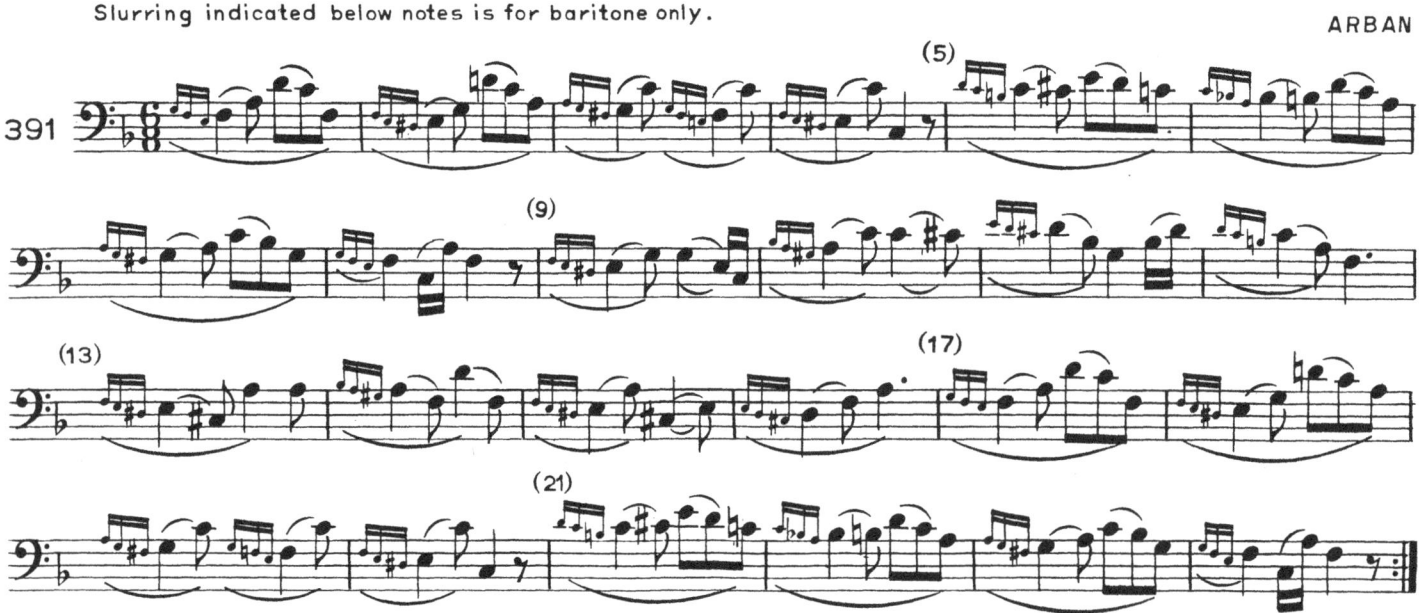

FOR BARITONE ONLY

The GRUPETTO (popularly known as a TURN) is a musical ornament consisting of a group of notes formed by the adjoining notes above and below the principal note, according to its position in the diatonic scale. It is indicated by the sign ∽ and is used in different ways.

ARBAN GRUPETTO STUDY No.1

ARBAN GRUPETTO STUDY No.2

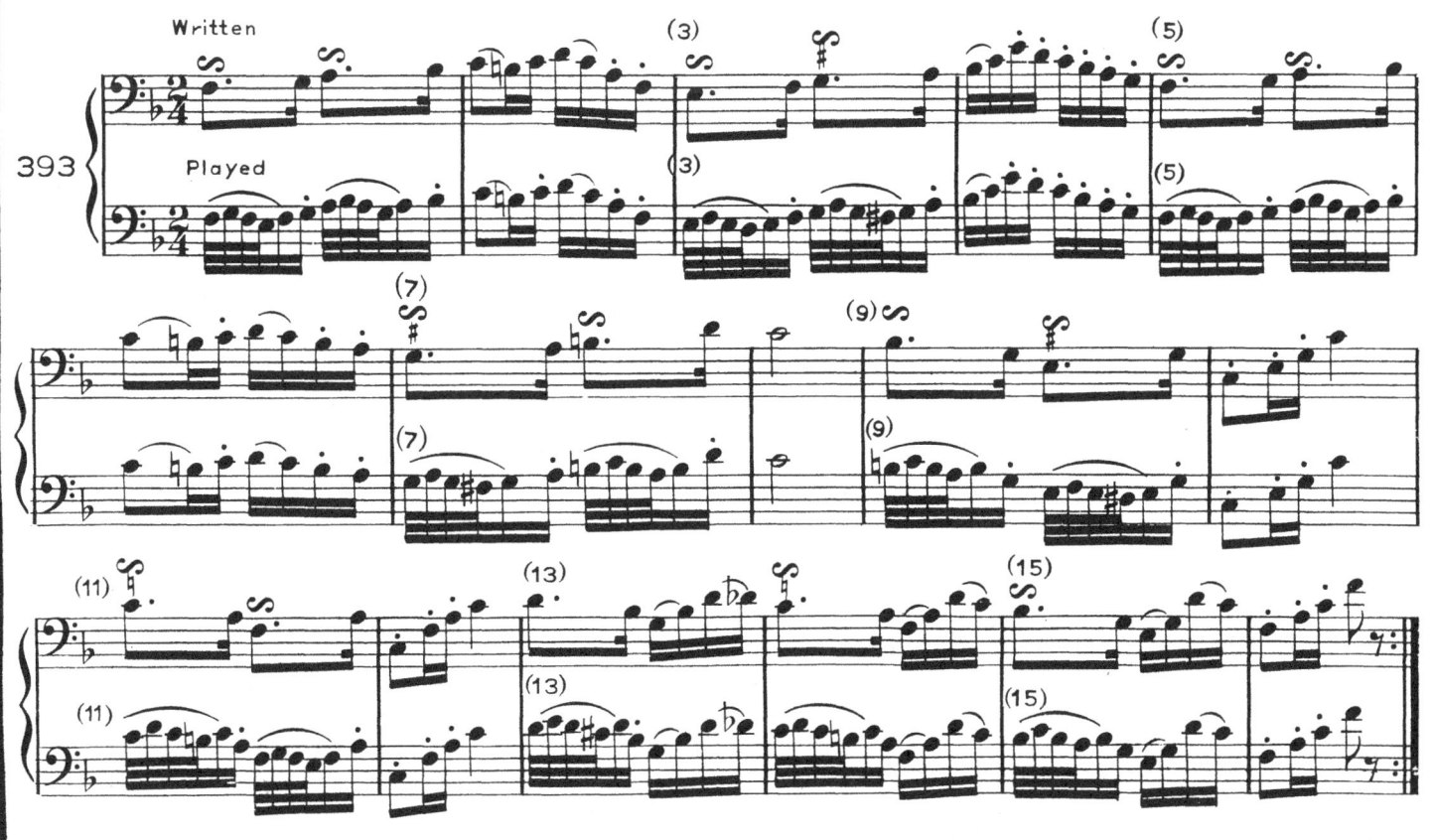

FOR BARITONE ONLY

The TRILL (sometimes called a Shake) is the most commonly used embellishment in music. It is an ornamental effect produced by the rapid and regular alterations of two tones, either a whole step or a half-step apart, and is indicated by the letter *tr* above the principal note, the alternate being the one above it. It does not matter how many notes a trill contains; the greater the number of notes in a trill, the more life and brilliancy the embellishment will radiate.

ARBAN TRILL ETUDE

FOR BARITONE ONLY

St. Jacome Complete Table of Trills
(Basic Exercises)

E = Easy   D = Difficult   ⊕ = Hardly practicable

Practice each exercise many times.

Not to be practiced until after having studied page 104

FOR BARITONE ONLY

The MORDANT (sometimes called a Passing Shake) is, in its most commonly played form, a double grace note embellishment consisting of the principal note alternated with a note above it. The sign ⁓ placed over a note indicates the mordant.

MORDANT STUDY

ST. JACOME EMBELLISHMENT ETUDE

Key of A Minor
(Relative to the Key of C Major)

Scale of A Harmonic Minor   Scale of A Melodic Minor

Also practice very slowly, holding each tone for (1) FOUR counts and (2) EIGHT counts.
When playing long tones, practice (1) < and (2) < >.

ST. JACOME ETUDE IN A MINOR

SONG OF THE VOLGA BOATMAN

Russian Folk Song

Key of D Minor
(Relative to the Key of F Major)

ST. JACOME ETUDE IN D MINOR

SERENADE
SCHUBERT

Key of E Minor
(Relative to the Key of G Major)

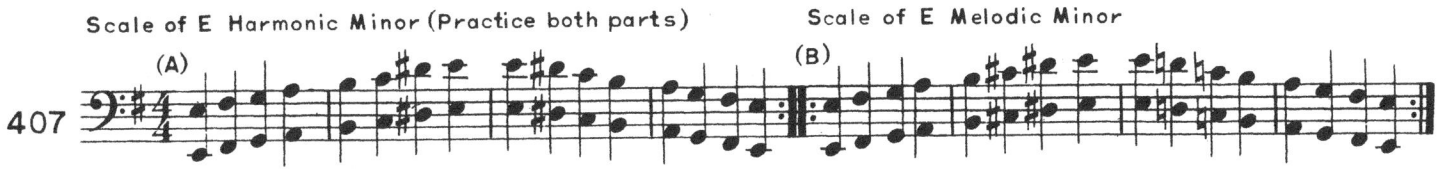

Scale of E Harmonic Minor (Practice both parts)   Scale of E Melodic Minor

Also practice very slowly, holding each tone for (1) FOUR counts and (2) EIGHT counts.
When playing long tones, practice (1) $\prec$ and (2) $\prec \succ$

ST. JACOME ETUDE IN E MINOR

CHANSON TRISTE

TSCHAIKOWSKY

Key of B Minor
(Relative to the Key of D Major)

Scale of B Harmonic Minor　　　　　　　　Scale of B Melodic Minor

413

Also practice very slowly, holding each tone for (1) FOUR counts and (2) EIGHT counts.
When playing long tones, practice (1) < and (2) <>.

ST. JACOME ETUDE IN B MINOR

414

NIGHT WINDS

TSCHAIKOWSKY
Op. 30, No. 24

415

Key of C Minor
(Relative to the Key of E♭ Major)

Also practice very slowly, holding each tone for (1) FOUR counts and (2) EIGHT counts.
When playing long tones, practice (1) ⟨ and (2) ⟨ ⟩

ST. JACOME ETUDE IN C MINOR

NATIVE HOMELAND

Folk Song

Key of F# Minor
(Relative to the Key of A Major)

Also practice very slowly, holding each tone for (1) FOUR counts and (2) EIGHT counts.
When playing long tones, practice (1) < and (2) < >.

ST. JACOME ETUDE IN F# MINOR

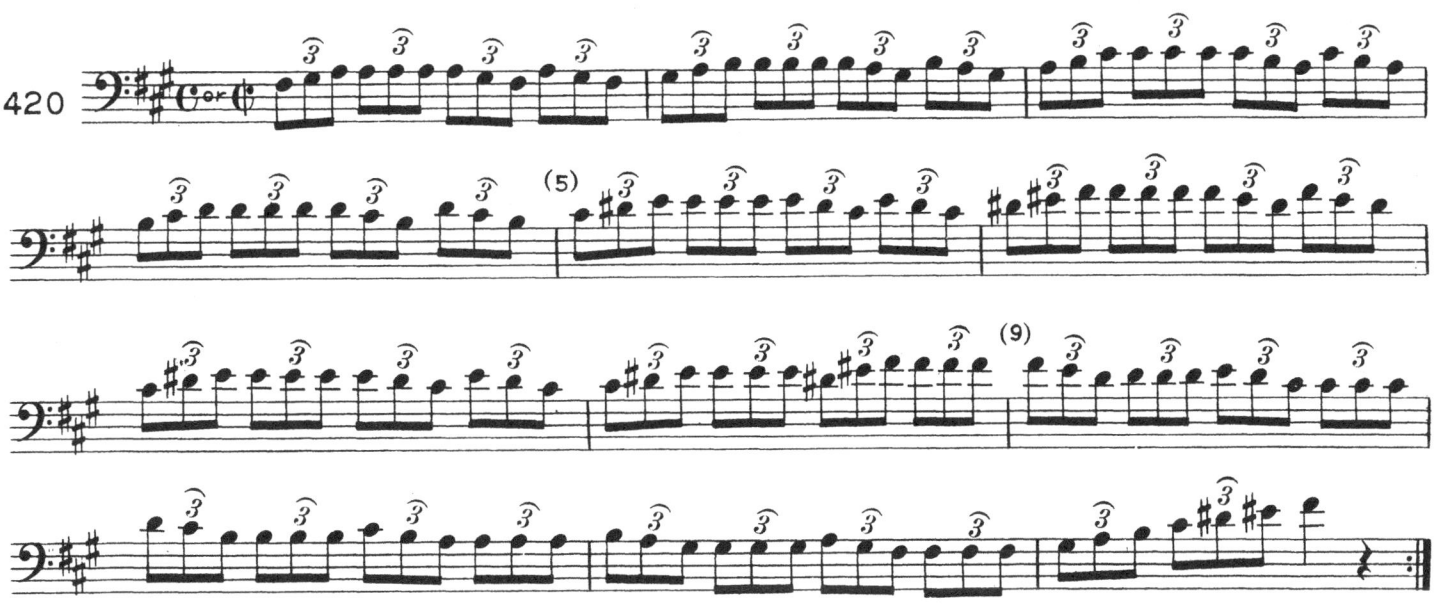

ELEGIE
MASSENET

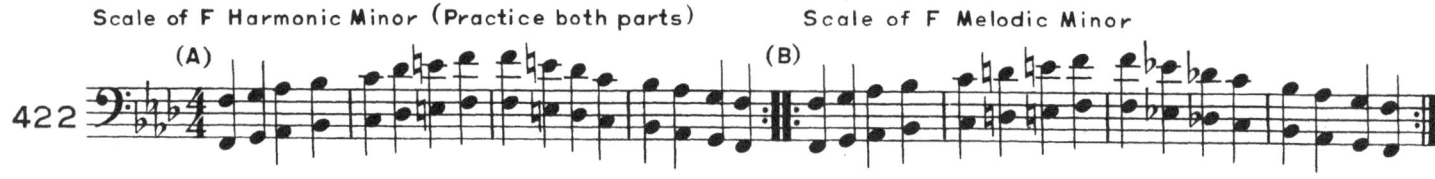

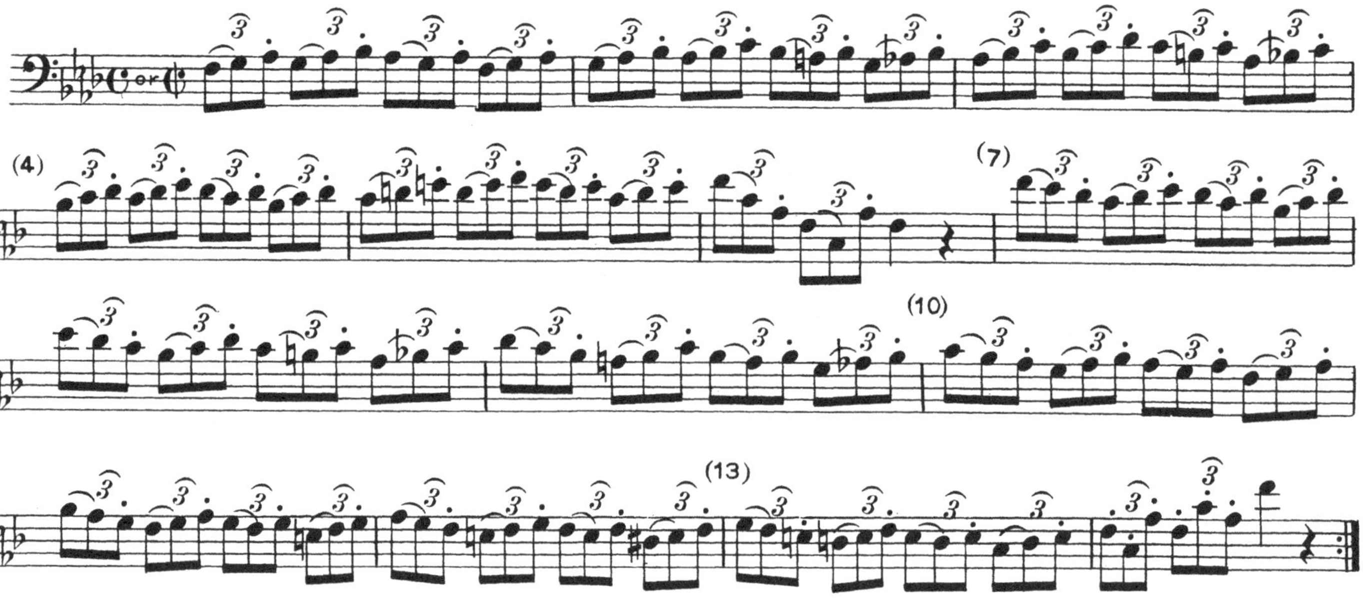

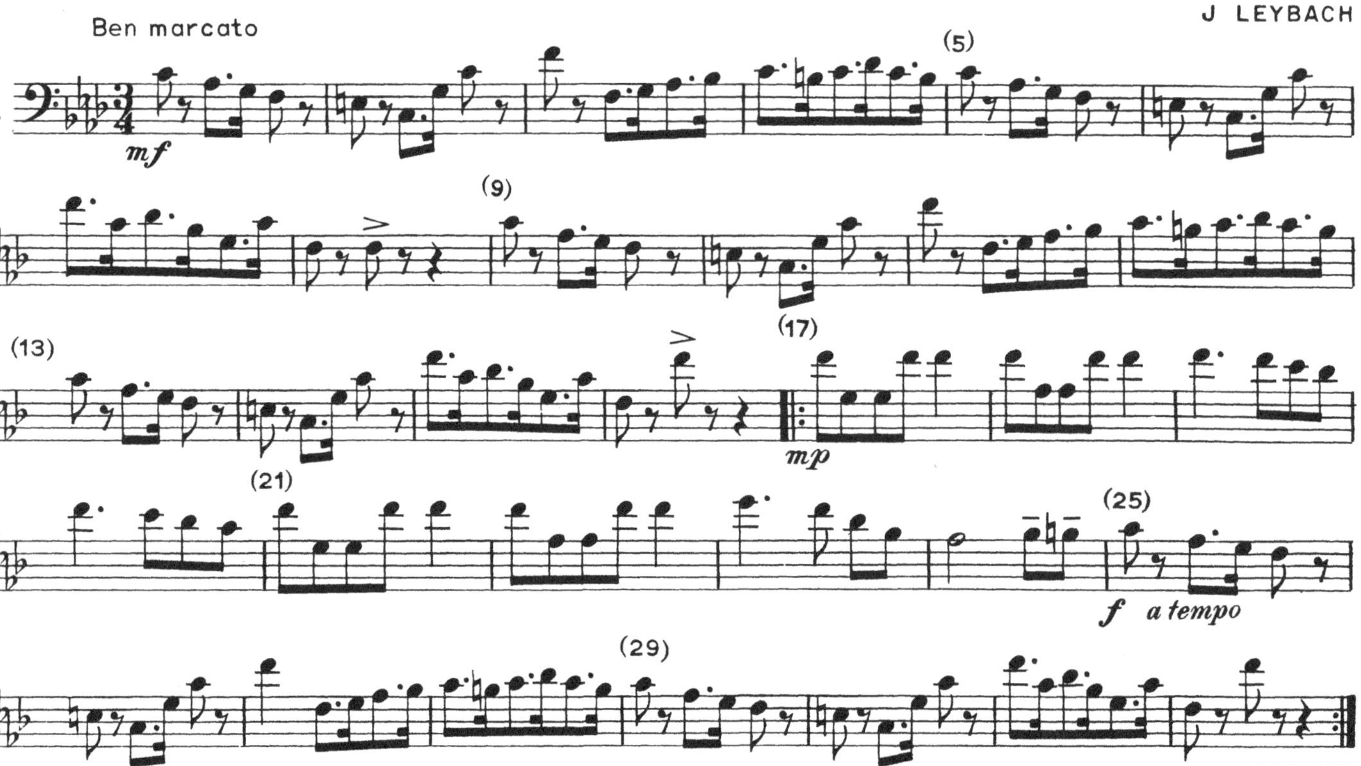

Key of B♭ Minor
(Relative to the Key of D♭ Major)

Also practice very slowly, holding each tone for (1) FOUR counts and (2) EIGHT counts.
When playing long tones, practice (1) ⟨ and (2) ⟨⟩.

ST. JACOME ETUDE IN B♭ MINOR

SYMPHONIC CAPRICE

CAMPANARI

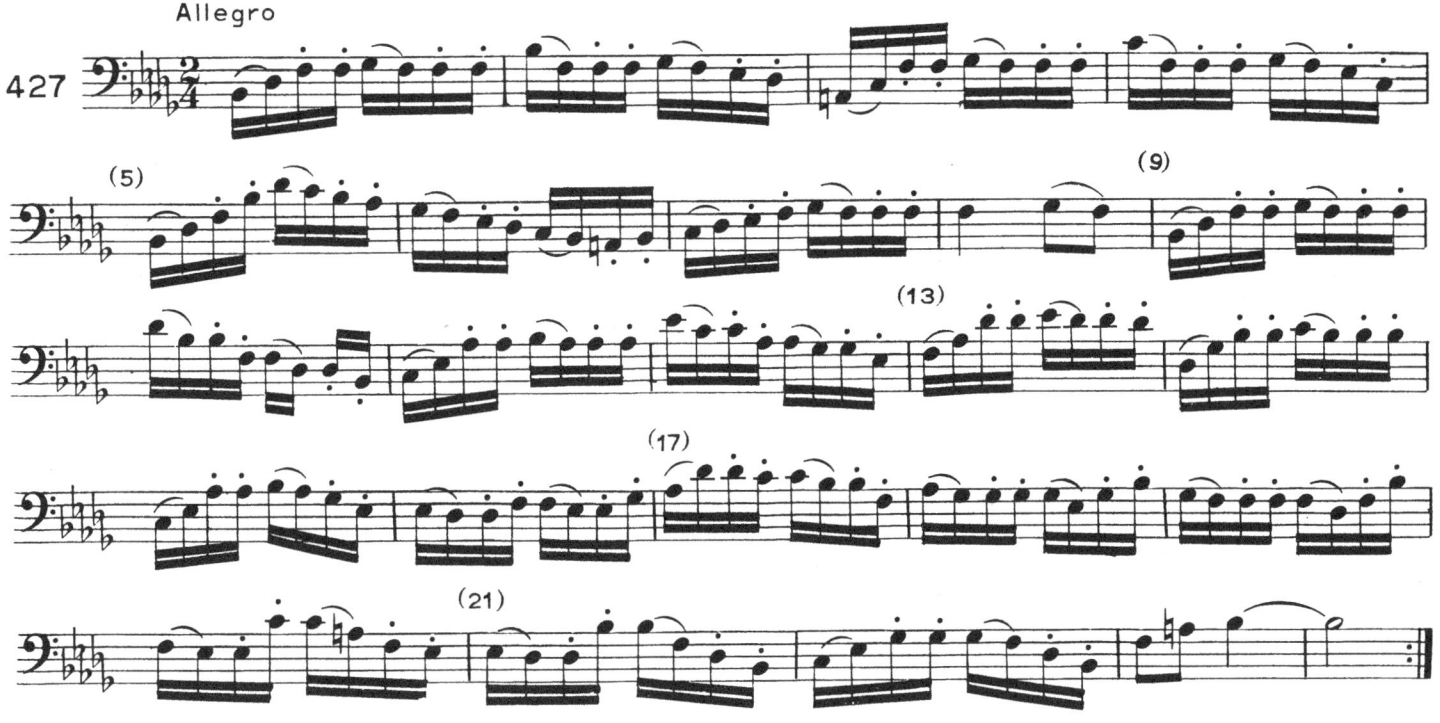

St. Jacome Advanced Interval Exercises

FIFTHS and SIXTHS

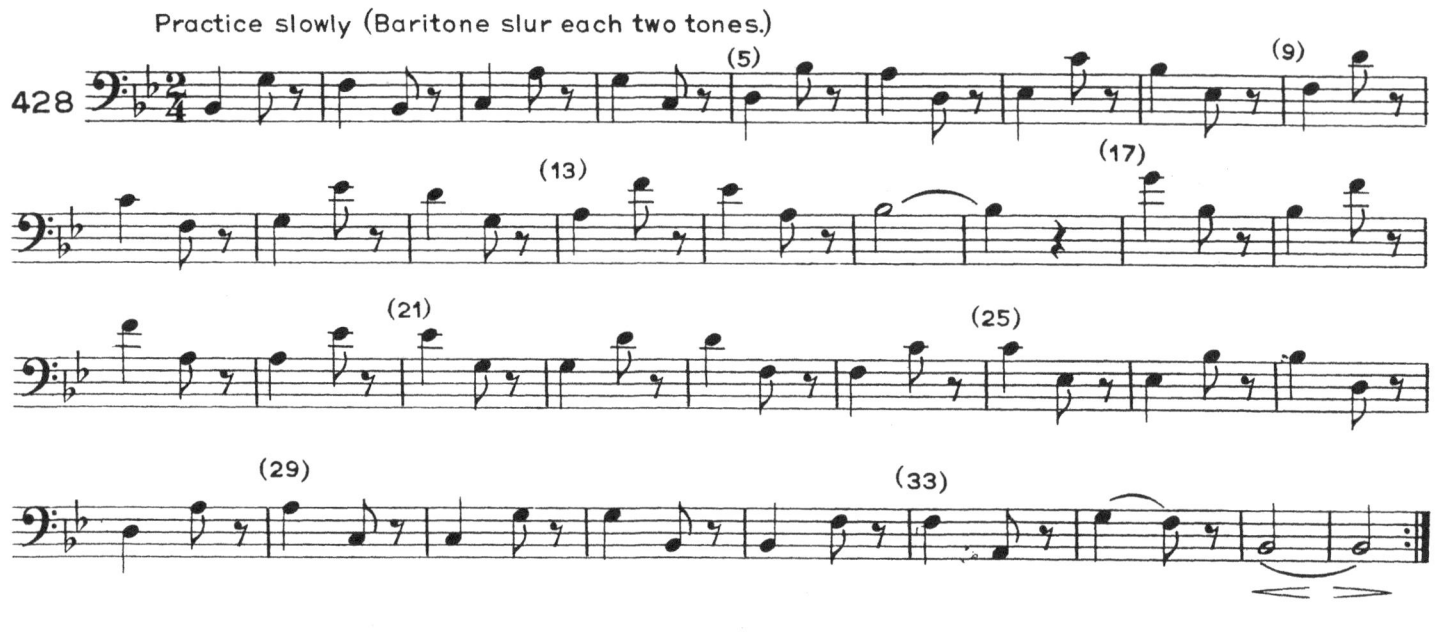

SIXTHS and SEVENTHS

OCTAVES

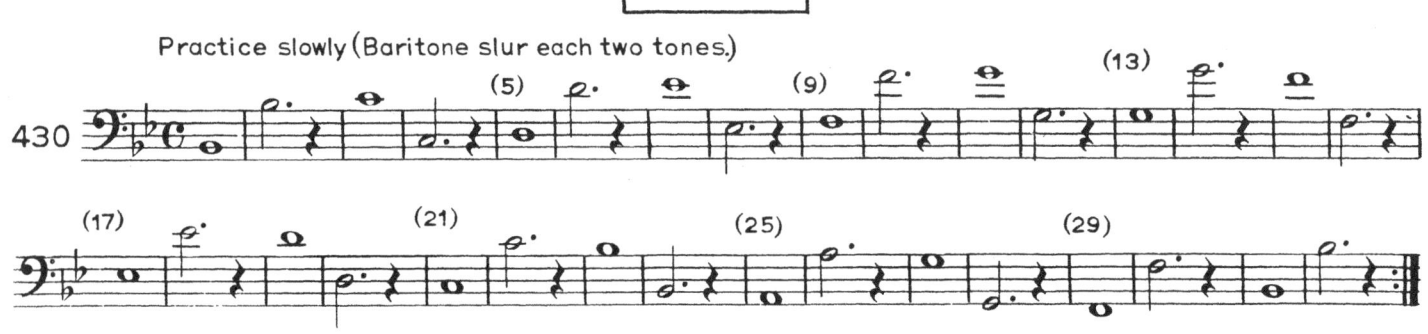

St. Jacome Chromatic Studies
SCALE EXERCISE

Practice in both Common and Alla Breve time.

INTERVAL EXERCISE

Practice in both Common and Alla Breve time.
Also practice (1) slurring each TWO tones, (2) slurring each FOUR tones, and (3) slurring each EIGHT tones.

Triple Tonguing

Triple Tongue Patterns
To be practiced on St. Jacome Articulation
Studies (Nos. 312, 313, 314, 315, 316, 317, 318, 319, 320), Pages 64-65.

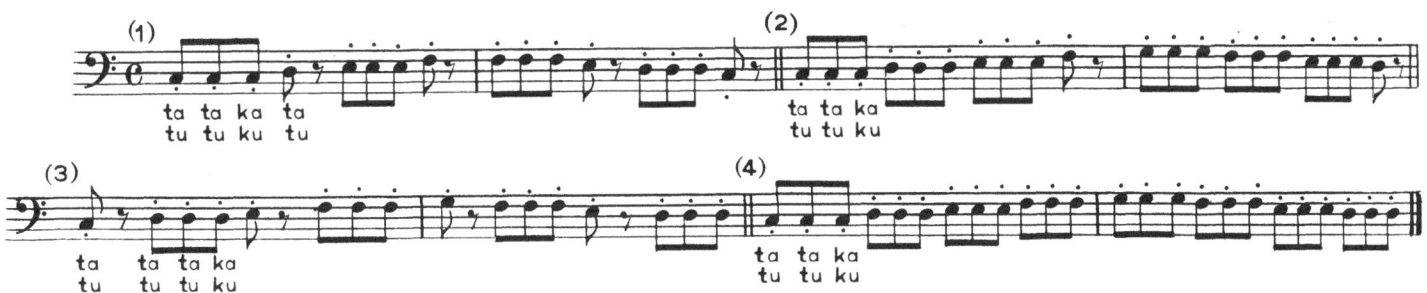

Polka Brilliant
from La Fille de Madam Angot

J. LEYBACH
Op. 169

Double Tonguing

Developing High Tones

INTRODUCING HIGH "G#-Ab"

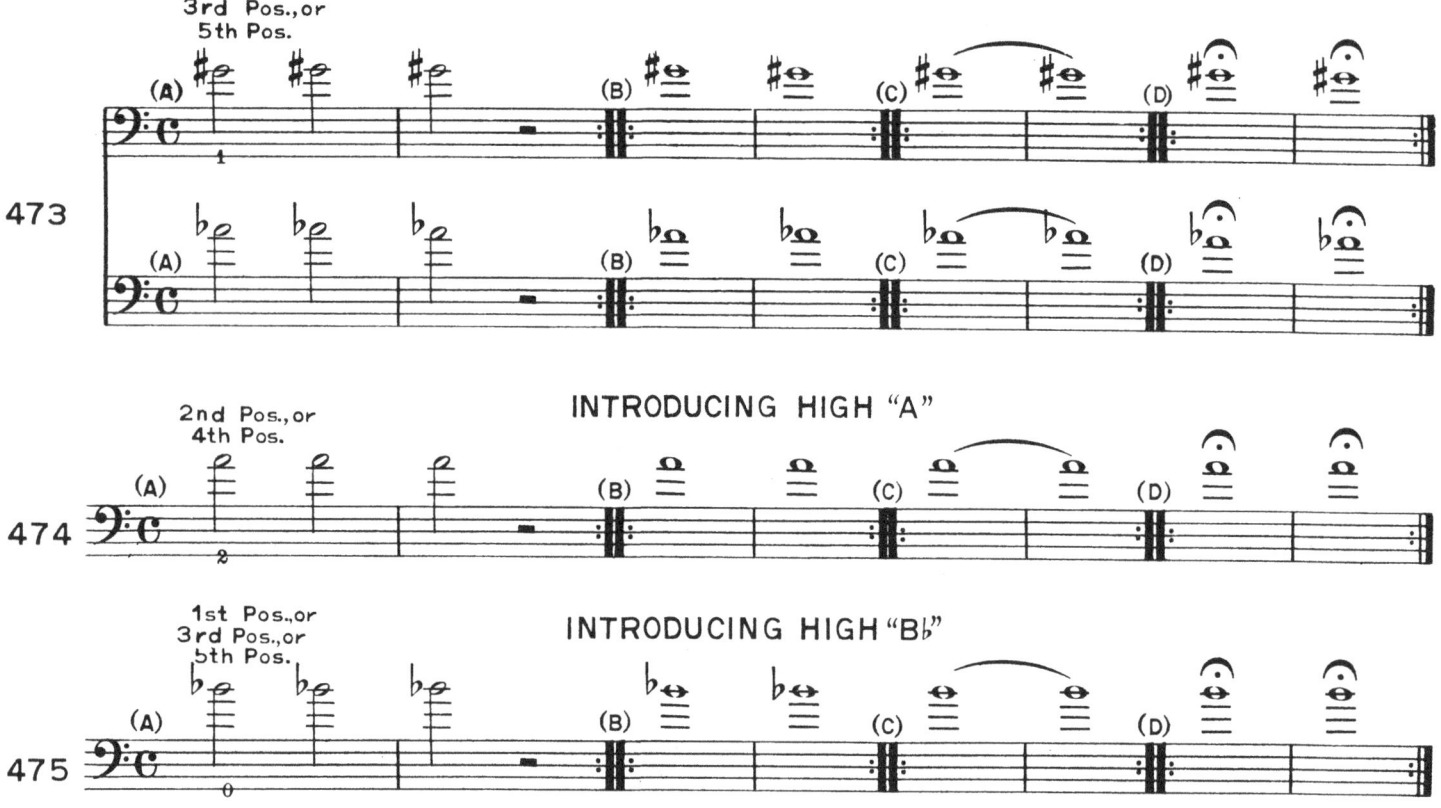

Short Studies in the High Register

(A) Also practice very slowly, holding each tone for (1) FOUR counts and (2) EIGHT counts. When playing long tones, practice (1) =< and (2) =< >=.

(B) BARITONE PLAYERS: Also practice very legato, (1) slurring each two tones, (2) slurring each four tones, and (3) slurring each eight tones.

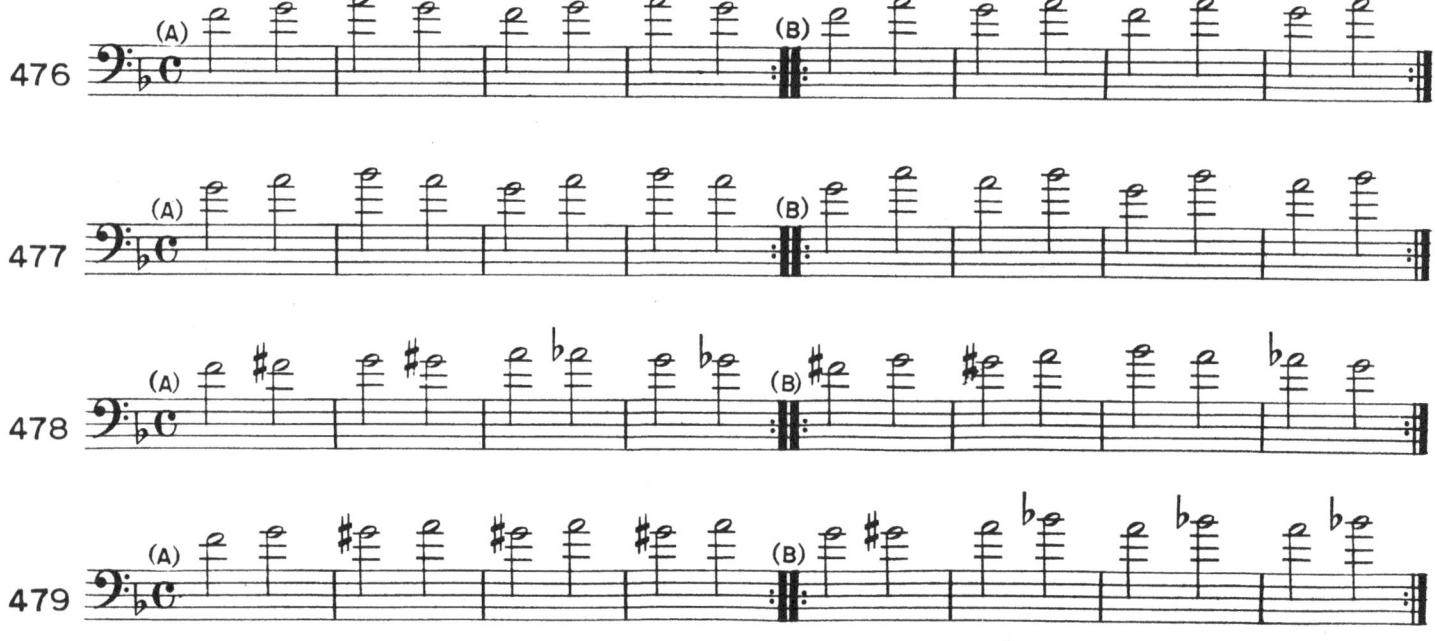